POTTERY BARN

storage & display

TEXT

martha fay
carol endler sterbenz
genevieve a. sterbenz

PHOTOGRAPHY

stefano massei

STYLING

deborah mclean
alistair turnbull

EXECUTIVE EDITOR

clay ide

Oxmoor House®

Oxmoor House

Oxmoor House books are distributed by Sunset Books
80 Willow Road, Menlo Park, CA 94025

Oxmoor House and Sunset Books are divisions of
Southern Progress Corporation

SUNSET BOOKS

Vice President, General Manager Rich Smeby
Vice President, Editorial Director Bob Doyle
National Account Manager Brad Moses

POTTERY BARN

President Laura Alber
Senior Vice President, Design & Product Development Celia Tejada
Vice President, Creative Services Clay Ide
Editor Samantha Moss Burggrabe
Photo Coordinator, Special Projects Forrest Stilin

WELDON OWEN

Chief Executive Officer John Owen
President & Chief Operating Officer Terry Newell
Vice President, International Sales Stuart Laurence

Creative Director Gaye Allen
Vice President, Publisher Roger Shaw
Business Manager Richard Van Oosterhout

Associate Publisher Shawna Mullen
Art Directors Joseph DeLeo, Colin Wheatland
Managing Editor Sarah Lynch
Production Director Chris Hemesath
Photo Coordinator Elizabeth Lazich

Pottery Barn Storage & Display was conceived and produced by
Weldon Owen Inc.
814 Montgomery Street, San Francisco, CA 94133
in collaboration with Pottery Barn
3250 Van Ness Avenue, San Francisco, CA 94109

Set in Simoncini Garamond™ and Formata™

Color separations by International Color Services
Printed in Singapore by Tien Wah Press (Pte.) Ltd.

A WELDON OWEN PRODUCTION

First printed 2004
10 9 8 7 6 5 4 3 2 1

Library of Congress Control Number 2003115876
ISBN 0-8487-2762-2

The Art of Organization

Storage and display satisfy two essential human instincts. On the one hand is the desire to create order, which explains the universal appeal of "a place for everything and everything in its place." On the other is the pleasure that comes from being surrounded by the objects that define our place in the world – family photographs, art collections, favorite books. In our homes, a balance of both invites us to fully appreciate the simple beauty of everyday objects, from a rustic wooden bowl to a sunlit display of glass vases.

At Pottery Barn, we believe in the value of creative solutions that make your home more organized and comfortable. Our approach is to provide inspiration and a wealth of options you can choose from to suit you, your family, and your own unique living space; this book is designed to assist you along the way. All of our photography is shot in real homes, so that what you see in these pages are accessible ideas to help you organize your life and enjoy it to the fullest. The information presented here can be easily adapted to rooms of all different sizes, shapes, and uses. In *Pottery Barn Storage & Display*, you'll find inspiration for every room in your house, and practical wisdom you can use to translate your creative ideas into stylish solutions.

THE POTTERY BARN DESIGN TEAM

contents

10 making room

22 entryways

90 bedrooms

106 closets

34 living rooms   56 family rooms   74 kitchens

124 bathrooms   150 laundry rooms   164 utility rooms

182 room resources
186 glossary
188 index
192 acknowledgments

making room

From the passionate collector to the avowed minimalist, all of us have many things to store – and many to display. If you strike just the right balance between the two, you can make your home more attractive and even improve your quality of life. Good storage streamlines everyday activities. It makes you more efficient and, at the same time, it makes your space more comfortable. Display, whether useful or purely decorative, is the natural complement to storage. An attractive display adds personality to a room, and makes it welcoming and inspiring.

Next, learn how to put unused areas of your home to work for you. As anyone who has packed a suitcase knows, it's not how much space you have, it's what you do with it. Learn to make the most of every inch at your disposal. By stacking books vertically as well as horizontally, you can reclaim space in shelving units with adjustable shelves. Invent extra storage by installing shelves and cubbies beneath windows, in corners, above doorways, and along hallways. And don't forget about wall hooks and hanging racks – they can swiftly create storage space out of an empty wall.

Life is so much better when everything is in its place. Living easily with treasured possessions – and everyday ones – simply requires organization and imagination.

Both storage and display require thought and organization. Although there is no foolproof way to create harmony in your space, there are a few practical strategies that can help simplify the process. Begin with the basic storage formula of subtraction and addition: reduce what you need to store, and find clever ways to add storage space throughout your home. First, streamline your belongings. Eliminate clothing that you never wear. Review items packed in long-term storage and give away what you can. Mementos take up more room than you might imagine, so use this simple criterion: if you love it, keep it. If you are not sure what to do with it, pass it on.

Finally, consider where and how you place your belongings. Do things accumulate on furnishings or pile on counters? Choose a commonsense system that suits what you do in each space. If you have plenty of closets and shelves but the floor is a magnet for clutter, install hooks or pegs to catch things before they land. If surfaces are the problem, bins and baskets are the solution.

Above all, remember that storage doesn't always have to be boxes and files. Creating a sense of order can be an imaginative process. If possible, sidestep the expected and choose interesting forms in place of standard storage. Trunks, woven baskets, and antique valises work just as well as more ordinary types of storage. They can also contribute to the overall design scheme, making storage an element of display. The rooms we love and remember most vividly are infused with personality. They are filled with thoughtful choices and unique pairings that blur the line between storage and display. And, while symmetry and balance and are said to be the keys to a successful display, its true heart is the ability to create a place that entices people to linger.

In addition to being practical, storage should offer a measure of beauty. The things you see every day should delight you.

Tradition suggests that certain things belong in certain rooms and that furnishings and decor should be matched in a particular style. The first rule of display is to break all of these rules and have some fun. While there are a few tricks to arranging beautiful displays, chief among them is to simply rely on your own instincts. Beyond that, remember that the most memorable displays thrive on repetition and relationship.

Displaying items in multiples, or repeating basic shapes, creates more interest and elevates everyday objects to the status of artwork. A single colored glass bottle may not catch the eye, but a shelf full of them is bound to be admired. Think about relating pieces in a display by color and material as well as provenance. All-white displays can contain an eclectic assortment of treasures and still look clean and unified. The rich grain of wood or the smooth texture of porcelain might be the common thread linking many objects great and small. A varied collection of two- and three-dimensional artifacts, all dating from the same era, can create a vivid, layered presentation.

Collecting things to display is an adventure that is always open to us. It has a treasure hunt quality to it and a sense of memories in the making. As your family grows or the seasons change, your displays can evolve, too. In autumn, change the focus of a room with colorful leaves and objects collected from nature. Create a gallery wall of shadow boxes containing vacation mementos. Or, fill a wide wall with photos that follow the progress of a child as he or she grows up.

Display cannot be measured by worth. If an object brings back fond memories or just makes you smile, put it out to enjoy.

Take cues from seasoned collectors and make a still-life display centered around a favorite theme. Celebrate a wedding or anniversary by giving pride of place to framed photos and cherished gifts on a living room mantel. Or, let your display rely on repetition of a shape. Place a group of varied photographs – taken in different locations and at different times – in a series of matching frames to form a cohesive arrangement. Above all, use the need for storage and the art of display to imprint each room with your own unique story.

Botanical
Studies

Birds
of North
America

Balancing Storage and Display

Storage and display are two sides of the same coin: the sensible, tidy side that longs for order, and the flamboyant, show-it-off side that loves everything out where it can be seen. Sometimes you want more of one, sometimes more of the other; in every room, a good balance is the goal.

Few of us live in rooms that offer the perfect amount of storage. And all of us love to reinvent our surroundings with intriguing display. To make a room comfortable, yet truly your own, you need to balance the two. Both storage and display take a great deal of care and planning, and both strengthen the stylish impact of a space.

When it comes to storage, think less about managing the odds and ends of life and more in terms of an overall plan. At the start, storage is an editing process. The mantra of professional organizers is "condense and contain." Once you've cleared away all but the necessary items, create storage where things will fit and where you want to find them. It may sound obvious, but this straightforward process can change the way you look at – and arrange – an entire room. Choose a mix of closed and open storage to play down what's awkward and highlight what's beautiful. If a calming effect is your goal, arrange objects symmetrically – in bookcases or on opposite sides of a window or fireplace. If you prefer the unexpected, try an asymmetrical arrangement: a pair of shelves or ledges on one side of a sofa, a single one on the other side. If tranquility is what you have in mind, a subdued color palette is your best bet.

A Chinese-style glass vitrine, *left*, displays a found animal horn on top of first-edition books. Baskets store other mementos. **Built-in shelving**, *right*, becomes more than a bookcase; a display of souvenirs and family heirlooms makes it a living scrapbook. A white backdrop calls attention to the objects.

Elevating treasured items draws more attention to them. Employ interesting pedestals, such as architectural salvage, music stands, or a stack of books.

While most anything can be hung on a wall or arranged on a shelf, the art of display is in the presentation. The classic method is to group items by color, material, or theme. Or, follow the lead of galleries and dedicate a whole wall to display by installing built-in shelves or lining up several bookcases. Open up some shelf space in the middle to highlight your favorite objects and create a focal point. This central display area can feature a changing array of pieces from your collection, keeping the room fresh.

Seagrass baskets, *above*, punctuate a wall of bookcases and provide orderly breaks in the display. Baskets can hold objects that you prefer to keep from view or want to rotate into display later. **A collection of framed photographs**, *right*, hangs in an asymmetrical arrangement that makes an attractive counterpoint to the geometry of the shelving.

Color Palette

Colorful collections of books, photos, and mementos are best displayed against a neutral background. Here, walls wrapped in creamy white, textured wallpaper add a base layer of interest. Shades of deep red-brown, in the mahogany furnishings and Douglas fir ceiling, along with the caramel-colored leather club chair, add an element of warmth against the white walls. A floor of dark ebonized oak, covered with a richly patterned rug, visually anchors the room and highlights the tones in the wood picture frames.

A large gallery display of family photographs is an especially attractive way to infuse any room with warmth. To make a photo wall, place your favorite photographs in frames of different sizes and shapes and hang them in a mosaic pattern. Unify your gallery by frame or mat color or by selecting only black-and-white images. New acquisitions can be added to the arrangement until you have formed an overall shape that works (diamond and rectangular are both interesting options). Another approach is to create several groupings with smaller framed photographs. A gallery can also be arranged on a table, using easel-style frames. Or, simply set out a photo album and some labeled boxes of photos for everyone to enjoy.

Pedestal vases, *left*, become a different sort of "frame" in this personal gallery. When not filled with flowers, they contain keepsake photos and found items. **An archival storage box**, *above*, invites a closer look at an informal collection of photos.

Storage and Care

Framed photographs should be kept away from humidity and direct sunlight to prevent warping and fading. If you choose to mat your pictures, use museum-quality acid-free mats to help keep pictures from sticking to the glass.

Loose photographs can be damaged by fingerprints, scratches, dust, and creasing. Wear gloves when handling prints, and keep them bundled and wrapped in acid-free tissue paper in an archival storage box to protect them from fading.

Antique collectibles should be handled carefully and lifted by their strongest points when transported. Avoid hanging ceramic or glass with wire as it may scratch the surface. Polishing or rubbing gilded or iridescent glass or ceramics may damage the surface.

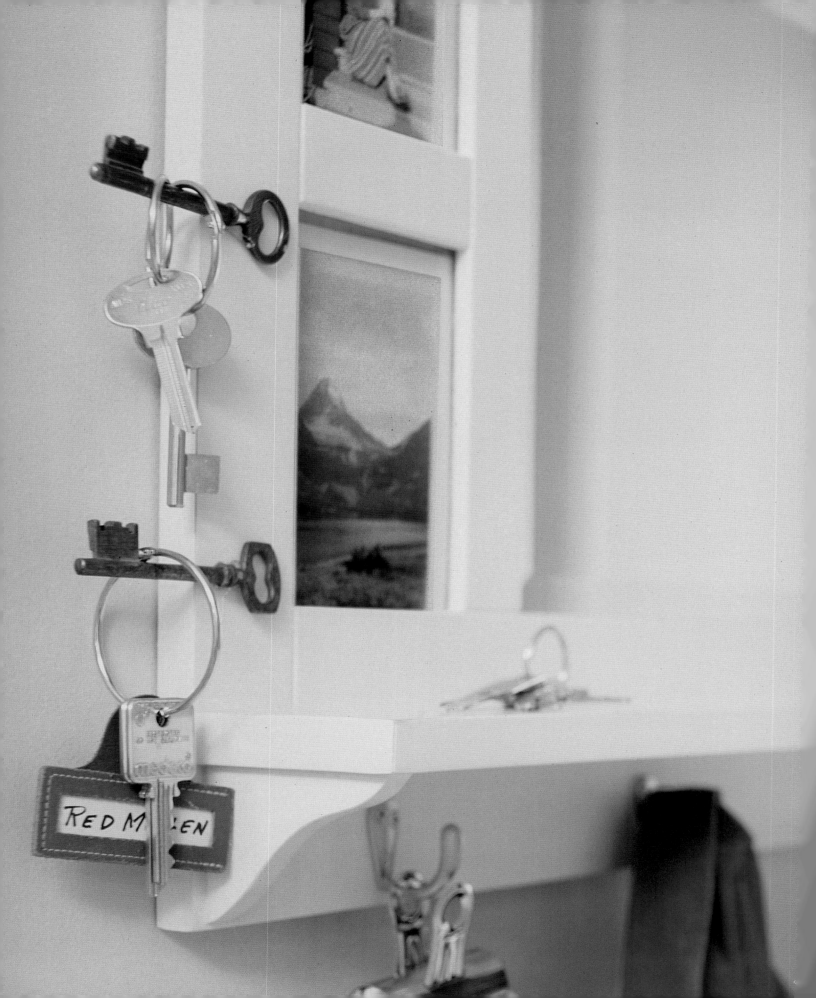

entryways

The entrance to your home tells a lot about you. Whatever its design style, it offers a first impression and sets the stage for the rest of the house. It can be a stylish greeting, a familiar haven, a place of welcome, or a natural place to display favorite objects.

For most of us, the entryway is a transition point as well and, thus, the natural home of the abandoned backpack, the wet umbrella, and the stack of mail that never made it to the kitchen. Important homework, mislaid glasses, pocket change, and keys all find a home in the entryway.

it should offer a few of the traditional comforts of hospitality – a place for guests to sit and remove wet boots, an uncluttered surface on which to set a gift while removing a coat, a mirror to sneak in a quick glance, an umbrella stand or hook, a closet or coat rack. Use the walls as well as the floor space when creating extra storage. Add shelves, with hooks for coats below and cubbies above, to bring order to a busy entryway.

As a practical matter, an entryway should also provide abundant storage for family members to stash their belongings when they return home.

An entryway can set the stage and make a serene and welcoming first impression. But first you have to stow away all the little things that a busy life demands.

Just as the living room requires an artful balance of both style and comfort, organizing a beautiful entrance to your home is about reconciling its two quite different uses: one as a well-trafficked space for daily comings and goings, the other as a decorative statement. Making your entryway work requires attention to where things tend to accumulate and what kinds of things they are. The goal is to find storage solutions that are as pleasing to look at as they are easy to use.

Ideally, an entrance should make a handsome first impression, a welcoming sweep of open space, something lovely and interesting to draw the eye forward into the house. At the same time,

A variety of storage systems makes the most sense: closed storage for seasonal or rarely used items, open containers for everyday items like bicycle helmets, mail, keys, and the dog's leash. A table-height cupboard or hutch that combines open shelves with closed storage is one practical idea. If space is tight, consider a narrow floor-to-ceiling bookcase fitted with removable baskets or bins that allow each person to store his or her possessions and find them again quickly.

When seeking places to keep things, think of convenience first. After all, the entrance to your home should be as welcoming for the people who live there as it is for the people who come to visit.

Elements of an Entryway

The secret to effective storage in an entryway is specialization. Provide enough appropriate containers – and enough broad hints – and keys and mittens will find their way to the proper places. The more conspicuous and accessible storage is, the more likely it is to be used.

An entryway generally leads a double life: it's part loading zone, part living room. It's where you and your family land after a busy day, where every instinct tells you to drop your gear and head for comfort. It's also where you greet guests, and the place from which you launch yourself back into the world the next day. But first, you have to find the car keys.

Because entryway storage is mostly short term – the things you use, and lose, every day – the key to maintaining order is making it easy and automatic. For optimum family cooperation, place storage at every level: hooks to hang hats and jackets, a table for mail and keys, a bin for boots on the floor, a side table to accept a briefcase or backpack at the end of a long day. When it comes to smaller items, little containers – single-purpose catchalls meant to receive the clutter of a busy household – go a long way toward taming the chaos of an entry hall. Open receptacles are easiest for people to make use of without having to stop and think; car keys go in the blue bowl, cell phone in the white one. Grouped together on a tray or shallow basket, your lineup of cachepots can be stashed out of sight and replaced with a vase of fresh flowers when company comes.

A tray full of small pots, *left*, keeps items like keys, pocket change, and dog-walking supplies sorted and in their place. **Baskets and benches**, *right*, are the perfect entryway pairing. Other essentials include hooks for coats, a place for wet things, and a durable floor mat or runner.

Dividing storage vessels by contents, or dedicating one to each family member, makes them much more likely to be used. Instead of one or two drawers for stowing clutter at the end of the day, offer containers in many shapes and sizes. Borrow from the garden, kitchen, or even the art studio. Sturdy wooden gathering baskets travel inside or out with equal ease. Kitchen trays can keep unsorted mail, or a collection of small containers, neat. Ceramic painter's cups are ideal for keys, glasses, pencils, and loose change. Remember that out of sight is usually out of mind: any receptacle left in plain view is far more likely to be filled than one hidden from sight.

A collection of weekend hats, *left*, makes a breezy display by the door and keeps them out where they'll be used. **A wooden carpenter's caddy**, *above*, becomes a handy carryall for organizing and transporting tools in and out of the garden.

Design Details

Color Palette

The inviting atmosphere of an entryway relies upon its color palette. Pale tints with a hint of warmth accented by bright, cheery hues are the best choice for a welcoming front or back entrance. Here, white walls and cream-colored furnishings create a feeling of airiness while wicker baskets and an intriguing collection of straw hats add warmth and texture to the room. A touch of sage green on the bench cushion and splashes of cheerful red and green help to turn an otherwise neutral palette into a welcoming color scheme.

Storage and Care

Outerwear should be hung on sturdy hooks or hangers. In a mudroom or entryway, wooden or iron pegs and hooks work best. Place them to accommodate all family members: stack the arrangement so that a hanger bar is available for adults, and pegs are below for small children.

Boots and shoes are best kept in durable storage along a back hall or tucked into a closet. Keep them organized with labeled bins, baskets, or built-in cubbies. Anticipate mud and puddles from rain boots and snow shoes with waterproof liners or trays.

Mittens and gloves should be stored near the entryway and sorted by size and user. Keeping them in baskets helps them dry quickly. Securing pairs with clothespins makes them easy to find. Baskets can be tucked into a closet or the framework of a console or set out as a winter display.

How to Create an Entryway Gallery

Entryways are irresistible locales for the display of family pictures and other treasured objects. Narrow passageways that might otherwise go unnoticed enjoy a second life as portrait galleries, celebrating a family's passions and history in a way that friends can share. Photographs are a natural choice for an entryway display, but so are children's first drawings, found objects, posters, and maps. When arranging your display, keep in mind the practical uses to which the space is put daily. Especially if you have a narrow entry, it's important to keep the floor area free for foot traffic, and to avoid bulky furniture that might get in the way of the display.

A narrow display shelf, *left,* is a simple idea for creating an instant entryway gallery. Here, red numbers from an old road sign share space with other decorative objects, creating a personal tableau that can be changed at will. The striking display has a practical side: below the shelf, wall hooks hold jackets, bags, and hats. **Transform a narrow hall**, *above,* into a space that has presence. A neat line of framed art captures the imagination. Grouping an odd number of items often makes for a successful display. **A staircase and landing**, *right,* can form a dramatic architectural backdrop for an entryway gallery. The large mirror on this landing heightens the drama and enlarges the space. Mount two shelves or ledges to create a stacked display, which lets you show more art in a small area.

How to Organize an Entryway

In-and-out traffic makes an entryway one of the busiest places in a home. It's the first place family members unload things, and the last stop on their way out the door. Why not take advantage of the entry's strategic location and transform it into a household communication command post? Notice the traffic patterns and daily habits of your household, whether it's large or small, and set up creative systems for sharing keys, sorting mail, and keeping belongings in place. Borrow an idea from wayside inns and use an old hotel key cubby as a family mailbox. All sorts of objects and containers can supply inspiration for your organization system.

A new take on a telephone table, *above*, this built-in storage unit turns an entryway into a place for cozy conversations and ends the frustration of racing to the ringing phone as you unlock the door. A full-size closet and a cabinet for telephone books make calling for your ride and putting on your coat a one-stop task. **A Victorian toast rack**, *right*, gets a practical update as a stylish perch for incoming or outgoing mail. A well-anchored coil spring would serve the same purpose just as well.

A vintage hotel lobby key box, *above*, finds useful new life as the family mailbox. Such a system can actually enhance household communication. Besides holding daily mail, it's a convenient place to post a notice, beg a favor, or leave a love note or birthday card. A galvanized tray, *left*, corrals footwear by the front door. Make a game of lining up shoes by size and you may even get a four-year-old to cooperate with your system. This tray is fitted with casters: when company is expected, just roll it out of sight.

living rooms

A living room blends the old with the new, opening a window onto a family's daily life and shared history. It's usually the biggest room in the home and the best dressed. Host to all sorts of everyday possessions, the living room is also a natural showcase for cherished family treasures – heirloom furnishings and keepsakes, or pictures that call for an honored place on the mantel or wall. In this room, ledges, shelves, bookcases, and tables are often in plentiful supply, making storage and display largely a matter of placement or container.

In a living room that does see daily use, traffic flow becomes especially important. Storage pieces, whether fixed or freestanding, can be used to help direct the flow. Floor-to-ceiling bookcases are ideal for large collections, and they also can help define a seating area or mark the break between a room's active and quiet zones.

Additionally, a room's existing architecture frequently offers unexpected opportunities for imaginative storage and display. A bay window is a natural site for a window seat with a capacious storage area underneath. A simple alcove, too

The living room is a place to share comforts and treasures with family and friends. Make room for both with imaginative storage that doubles as display.

Storage and display elements in your living room should be determined by how you use the room on a daily basis. Ask yourself what kinds of activities the room needs to accommodate. Identify your own preferences for open versus closed storage, styles of display, and degrees of visibility of everyday objects. Do you like the formality of built-in pieces, or do you prefer the flexibility of freestanding storage so that, when the mood strikes, you still have plenty of options? If the room doubles as the family library, open storage is a natural choice. If children use it daily or it is also the television room, storage that keeps clutter out of sight may be the best option.

shallow to accommodate a seating arrangement, might make a perfect self-contained library or compact gallery displayed on floating ledges. Narrow spaces between windows can be fitted with shelves to present favorite small collections. An unused corner of the room can be profitably reclaimed for storage with the addition of a slender curio cabinet or a vertical series of floating shelves, arranged floor to ceiling.

Remember that display is often storage made visible. Not everybody has a collection, but we all have things we want to stow and favorites we want to show off. In a well-planned living room, the right storage handsomely blends the two.

Living with Books

A library of books, collected over a lifetime, invites curiosity and stimulates the imagination. In a room dedicated to the pleasures of reading, a wall of well-loved books is not only a catalog of our interests and hobbies but also an attractive declaration of our passions.

Lined up on a shelf or stacked on the floor, books capture the imagination. Their varied sizes, colors, and textures tempt us to draw them out and turn their pages. Whether you have a few favorite volumes or enough to fill several walls, a book collection can be the foundation of a room's style and character. Organizing books offers a chance to combine storage with decor at every level of the room.

First, seek storage that allows flexibility, so you can easily change which volumes are kept at hand and which are put away. Don't hesitate to bring in furnishings commonly used for other purposes. A music stand is a nice way to display a book; an ottoman or long bench can become a casual library table. You may also want to have an easy way to identify a book's location in a collection. For books housed in a long wall of shelving, adopt the library custom of dividing and labeling each section by topic. Make handwritten signs to add a playful element. Try gardening stakes, clear picture frames, or even miniature chalkboards. For a personal touch, affix bookplates to the inside covers, or slip a short, dated comment or question about a book between the pages for the next reader who picks it up.

Miniature chalkboards, *left*, repurposed from garden stakes, categorize books by subject matter. Inserted between books, these handwritten signs are easy to move as a collection grows and changes. **A stack of books**, *right*, doubles as a side table and keeps reference books handy and in circulation.

Shelves offer infinite possibilities for arranging decorative still-life displays with books. You can paint the interior of the shelves in a rich color to draw attention to your collection and add depth and visual interest to the room. Sorting books according to their hue can make a colorful impact. It's an approach that offers a clean overall presentation and some interesting, and unlikely, subject pairings.

A wall of well-loved books is the simplest way to add warmth and character to your living room.

Pay attention to mixing shapes, too. Rocks and other organic objects from nature are a nice way to break up the geometric repetition of books on a shelf. Try topping horizontal stacks of books with a rock, a shell, or a fossil. Make special books a focal point by placing them face out so the jacket is on display, or fill an entire shelf with oversize books stacked flat.

Shelves create more space than they take up. Shelving need not be any deeper than fifteen inches to easily accommodate most book sizes. Good reading light (essential in any library) and comfortable armchairs pulled up to the fireside create a warm and welcoming place to enjoy the company of a book collection.

Bookcases can help create symmetry in a room, and can capitalize on every nook and cranny. If you have a bay window or a large doorway, balance its shape and enhance the drama by flanking it with a pair of bookshelves. When choosing ready-made shelves, invest in sturdy, solid construction and good wood veneers. Shelves that are devoted to books should be no more than forty inches long to keep them from sagging in the middle.

Built-in bookcases can help visually balance or disguise the asymmetry of a room's architecture.

If your collection is small or there's not enough room for shelves, you can still store your books to decorative advantage. Traditional nineteenth-century gentlemen's libraries always featured a library table. Usually crafted from mahogany, these wide worktables were large enough to lay out several books at once. You can create a library table of your own by setting out low stacks of books on a coffee table or ottoman.

A corner cabinet, *left*, offers deeper storage than shelving and a visual break in the wall of books. Artifacts and books, *right*, are arrayed on the generous surface of an ottoman, carrying on the tradition of the nineteenth-century library table.

Some books call out to be displayed and are meant to be preserved. They may be collector's volumes, favorites from childhood, or simply beautiful examples of the bookmaker's art. Whether hung on the wall or displayed on a table, deep shadow-box frames let you present books as artworks. Be sure to use an acid-free mat and mount the book between pins, rather than using glue, to preserve its value and keep it intact. Group related books within the same frame, or, if you own two of the same volume, display the front and back covers side by side.

A book of botanical prints, *left*, sits open on a bookstand for all to enjoy. On the wall, rare antique volumes are displayed in archival shadow boxes as fine art. **Leatherbound desk accessories**, *above*, are handsome keepers of antique manuscripts and books that have been wrapped in acid-free archival paper and neatly labeled.

Color Palette

An updated version of a classic library's color palette, this room combines rich tones of deep red and dark brown. The backdrop of buff yellow walls along with two chairs upholstered in natural cotton twill help make the atmosphere more casual. Traditionally painted in oxblood red or forest green and furnished with a blend of mahogany and leather, the classic library decor is referred to here but given a modern twist with a cognac leather ottoman, redwood shelving and woodwork, and floors of red granite.

Storage and Care

Hardcover books should be loosely packed on shelves – with large books stored flat – to avoid overcrowding. Use bookends for even support to prevent covers from warping. Keep all books away from humidity, and leave dust jackets on to protect the inside covers.

Leatherbound books should be kept at moderate temperature and humidity levels. Heat and dryness can crack tanned leather, and dampness can cause swelling and mildew in paper. Keep leatherbound books clean and free from pests with frequent vacuuming using a soft brush extension.

Antique books are most susceptible to damage due to mishandling, ink stains, paper clips, and exposure to light. Books that require archival storage should be kept in acid-free boxes; antiques should first be individually wrapped in acid-free tissue.

Creating a Treasure Wall

Display is as much a matter of the heart as it is a balance of shape and scale. Drawn from an expanding collection of art, books, objects, and photos, living room displays reflect the beauty and texture of our lives. Use built-in shelves to highlight your treasures and create a room full of discovery.

Over the years, an increasing number of books, photographs, and all sorts of mementos collect in the living room to form a rich scrapbook of experiences. Such a varied and prized collection demands a thoughtful display plan – one that will highlight favorite objects and reveal more of the collector's interests and experience with each new addition. One option is to fill an entire wall of shelves with objects of personal significance in the spirit of a traditional Chinese "treasure wall," whose small, square compartments held objects carefull organized by color, shape, and size to form a cohesive display.

With a skillful mix of editing and placement, you can create a treasure wall of your own. Group artifacts, books, mementos, and photographs to form creative vignettes for each shelf. Arrange pieces based on provenance, material, or size. Place heavy objects in the lowest shelves and lighter, more delicate items up high. Tell a story with a timeline of historic objects o make a sly remark with a few unlikely pairings. Paint the insid of shelves in a contrasting color to add the eye-catching depth of a shadow box to your treasure wall. Shelving offers limitles possibilities and a flexible framework for your favorite things.

A built-in media center, *left*, has sliding doors to hide away electronics and blend into the orderly grid of the "treasure wall." **Shelves become shadow boxes**, *right*, with a golden yellow hue painted on the inside to draw the eye to the contents of each cubby. Objects are arranged to present a casual, offhand sensibility with a mix of man-made and natural textures and shapes.

Design Details

Color Palette

The easiest way to call attention to a prized collection or bring harmony to a wall of shelving is to add color. Here, recessed storage is given visual order and interest with a coat of pale golden paint applied to the inside of each cubby. Set within a framework of crisp white walls and complemented with neutral furnishings, the yellow draws the eye and sets a series of stages for a display wall of life's treasures. The furnishings – upholstered in sand twill and dark brown leather – are subtle complements to the items on display.

Storage and Care

Architectural salvage is most beautiful when it's in relative disrepair. In order to keep crumbling pilasters and cracked pediments from degenerating too much, keep them securely out of harm's way and dust them with a soft feather duster.

Botanicals, such as dried leaves, cones, and flowers, should be kept in open containers, away from moisture. For long-term storage, wrap each item in tissue or newspaper and keep in a ventilated container. Store in a cool, dry room.

Ironstone is best kept on firmly anchored shelves. Stack the heaviest items on the bottom and place smaller pieces up high. For long-term storage, wrap each piece in bubble wrap and store in a cool, dry room. Make sure items are clean before storing, to prevent stains from setting in.

How to Organize Books

A well-loved book collection deserves pride of place in every home. Although storing books is largely a matter of keeping them in good condition and within easy reach, their arrangement can be decorative as well as practical. Whether you keep books upright or flat, open or closed, the way you store them should extend a sense of their valuable presence. Look at your books in a new way. They can become decorative accessories or free-form sculptures. Stack similar sizes or colors together, or build a graduated tower for a pyramid shape. Seek out unusual pedestals and elevated places to showcase favorite titles or a beloved book series.

Bureau drawers, *top*, rescue overflowing bookcases and protect books from dust and sunlight. Baskets are another option for hidden storage. **A music stand**, *above*, displays an illustrated volume left open to a favorite page. Antique lap desks, dictionary lecterns, and beautiful trays make intriguing book holders. **Design books**, *right*, can be stacked horizontally and their jackets appreciated in a whole new way.

Flanking a doorway, *left*, bookshelves can make the most of empty wall space. **Built-in bookcases**, *above*, stretching from floor to ceiling are a space-saving way to display a large collection. To soften the colorful effect of an entire wall of books, one trick is to remove all the dust jackets for a more neutral, subdued appearance. Another option is to hang sheer panels of fabric over the shelves.

How to Create a Photo Gallery

Make your walls more than a backdrop by assembling a perfect display with your favorite photos. Fill a large wall space with a collection of identically framed images, or create a dramatic display by mixing framed works with shadow boxes and three-dimensional items. As a general rule, hang frames at eye level (usually five feet or so from the floor) or slightly higher if you have high ceilings. Balance the size of the frame with the space: small frames may have more impact grouped together; large framed art can stand alone. With a little creativity, it's easy to transform an ordinary wall into your own personal gallery.

A colorful series of abstract paintings, *above*, can be unified by placing the pictures in frames of the same size and hanging them tightly together. This arrangement produces the impression of a single dramatic piece of art. Enlarging pictures with a color copier and framing them is another quick way to create a unique gallery display.

A photographic record of a special event, *right*, like a wedding or birthday, creates a display with style. Choose a wall location and place three equal-size frames in the center to establish a focal point. Add rows, grouping pictures an inch or two apart, to form a square or rectangle. For a graphic effect, use only black-and-white photographs or visit a copy center and change favorite color snapshots to black and white.

Framed artwork, *above*, doesn't always have to hang on a wall. Divide a group of pictures and present them spaced evenly apart on a ledge or along a hallway. For variety, stagger the frame heights or overlap a few images. Build a timeline of a family vacation, a growing child, or an important event by lining up framed pieces in chronological order. **Wooden clip hangers**, *left*, are an intriguing and quirky alternative to picture frames. Or, try clipping unframed pieces to a length of wire. Stairwells are good areas for photo displays; hang artwork following the upward angle of the stairs.

How to Hang Pictures

First, lay all of your artwork out on the floor and experiment until you find an arrangement you like. Multiple frames look best arranged in a rectangular, square, or diamond shape and set in a tight group, about an inch or two apart. A looser arrangement can also work for a more casual display. A straight line of pictures, whether horizontal or vertical, is timeless and sophisticated.

Transform several generations of family photos into an attractive gallery by displaying them on a single wall. Gather baby pictures and hang them in a timeline with frames touching. Start hanging from the left, and use a level to make sure each is straight before hanging the next. Make a collection of snapshots or informal pictures artful by giving them colorful mats and placing them in a vertical line. Once you've decided on the display you want, follow the instructions below to place hangers and mount pictures.

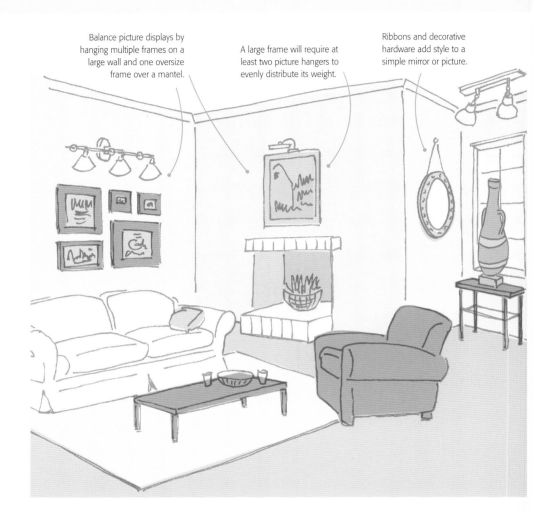

Balance picture displays by hanging multiple frames on a large wall and one oversize frame over a mantel.

A large frame will require at least two picture hangers to evenly distribute its weight.

Ribbons and decorative hardware add style to a simple mirror or picture.

How to hang multiple pictures Use paper outlines to help visualize and decide on the ideal arrangement. Place the center of the group at eye level. Use string stretched between two pushpins as a guide for hanging rows of frames.

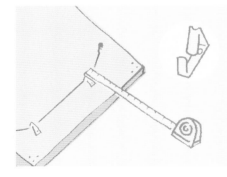

How to hang large pictures Two picture hangers will keep frames from tilting. Before nailing into a wall, measure the distance from the taut wire to the top of the frame. Use these measurements as a guide to affixing picture hangers on wall.

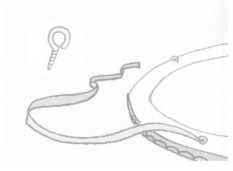

How to add a ribbon hanger Tie one end of a ribbon to an eye hook. Hold picture up to the wall and loop the free end of ribbon over a nail or decorative hanger. Adjust tautness until picture is at the desired height. Affix ribbon to the other side.

lighting your artwork to make the most of your display

Adjust the direction of gallery lights so the beams overlap.

Illuminate a large picture with a light attached directly to the frame.

Track lighting can direct light precisely onto artwork.

Use natural light from a window to backlight a sculpture during the day.

How to Light Picture Displays

Give your favorite artwork the spotlight it deserves with well-planned lighting. Picture lighting can be provided by fixtures mounted directly to the picture frame, on the wall above or below, or as track or spotlights on the ceiling. The goal is to provide even illumination across the entire surface of the image while protecting it from the lamp's heat. Low-wattage halogen, which tends to be most color-correct, is perfect for lighting art.

Pay attention to the height of the room and the height of the artwork. If the artwork is tall, a ceiling-mounted light should be placed close to the wall to illuminate the entire piece. Select a fixture color for track lighting or gallery lights that is as close to the wall color as possible, so that fixtures don't detract from the artwork. Use a bulb at least three times brighter than the overall light in the room to draw attention to objects such as sculptures.

How to light multiple frames Match the width of the light beam – wide or narrow – to the size of your artwork, in order to make it stand out. Evenly illuminate a large arrangement with multiple wall-hung fixtures and overlapping arcs of light.

How to position a frame-mounted light Lights should be suspended approximately 8 inches from the surface of the artwork. Seek designs that are well shaded. Battery-powered models make it easy to change the location of the art.

How to adjust ceiling lights Spotlights and track lights have pivoting arms to help guide the light to just the right angle. Use narrow-beam halogen bulbs to focus pools of light directly onto objects. This will also help reduce glare.

family rooms

Casual comfort is the spirit of a family room. Its mood is informal and cozy, making it the perfect place to watch television or listen to music, to roam the web or tell a story. It's also the ideal spot for showing off collections, family pictures, and artwork you love. In short, it's a room in need of well-organized storage that leaves plenty of space for display.

With books, CDs, DVDs, toys, and video games all in play, keeping a family room orderly takes dedication – and a lot more knowledge than it once did. If you have any kind of a collection,

The television is the largest item needing storage in the family room. Whether it's the room's focal point or concealed within a media center, it should be stored in a spot that allows for optimal viewing. Stereos and other electronics present a different challenge: their cords and wires should be tucked away for safety, as well as aesthetic reasons. Keep in mind that electronics emit heat and, in closed storage, will need room to breathe.

Make it easy for the whole family to relax by maximizing accessibility, storing toys within easy reach for children, movies near the television,

Order encourages harmony. In a room designed for relaxation, an organized storage system is as crucial to family happiness as spending time together.

you know that you need the skill of a librarian to stay on top of things. You want an efficient system to keep track of books and all the other entertainments (including the remote), because storage in this room is all about ease of use.

A beautiful wall of books is twice as beautiful to a family of readers if it follows some organizing principle. You might file fiction alphabetically by author, arrange reference volumes on a single or adjacent shelves, and keep history in one section and travel writing in another. Shelve standard-sized books spine out; and place large, coffee-table books flat on a shelf, three or four to a stack, to add interest to your bookcase display.

music near the stereo, and all remote controls in a dedicated spot. For storing DVDs and videos, any easily accessed container – a vintage trunk, a basket under the coffee table – will do, as long as you stick to a system of clearly labeling the boxes and keeping them filed label-side out.

Periodically weed out your collections. Your local library will welcome used books, CDs, DVDs, and videos that are in good condition. Board games and toys that are only taking up shelf space could find happier homes at a school or daycare center. Meanwhile, back at your house, having a place for everything and keeping everything in its place makes all the difference.

Cool, Calm, and Collected

Even with plenty of storage, an active family room needs help staying organized. Transform a busy den into family headquarters with drawers and containers highlighted in fresh hues and color-coded for each family member. After all, a little order is a wonderful thing.

Imagine a family room that gracefully balances storage and style, a comfortable place where people like to collect but clutter doesn't. With a few twists on traditional storage, it's easy to increase your family room's comfort quotient and keep it looking neat at the same time. In a space where schoolwork, office work, games, and projects compete for every inch, it's a challenge to maintain a sense of order. One tactic is to concentrate storage along a wall (whether with fitted or freestanding shelves and cabinets) and color-code containers for each family member. This approach encourages neatness and leaves room for camaraderie.

If you're remodeling or building, consider including a wall unit in the family room, to provide both storage and activity space. Otherwise, furniture with good storage potential is essential: use a steamer trunk as a coffee table, or choose a coffee table with compartments and slip matching bins or baskets into its framework. To individualize the storage for each family member, continue the color-coding system. This way, everyone's things are easy to find, no matter who put them away last, and cleanup goes more quickly.

Empty space becomes extra storage, *left*, with roomy boxes sized to slip into the open framework of a coffee table. Everyone in the house is assigned their own color. **A central built-in cabinet**, *right*, conceals a media center behind its doors. The cupboard above stores instructions, guides, and paperwork; lower drawers hold movies, games, and toys.

Placing all the cabinets and drawers along a single wall offers several benefits. Painted to match the rest of the room, the storage seems to disappear. When the doors of the center cabinet are open, the television or stereo becomes the focal point. The built-ins in this room establish several activity zones while keeping pathways clear. A multiuse home office sits to one side, ready for bill paying or homework. The other end of the unit supplies a project area, with inventive displays to spark the imagination.

Toy storage, *above*, swings out from lower cabinet doors so kids can reach toys and clean up by themselves. Under the desk, stacking boxes provide more child-friendly storage space. **An indoor garden**, *right*, set on toy trucks, makes both a whimsical display and a learning opportunity. Magazine racks mounted on both sides of the media cabinet hold children's books.

Design Details

Children's books stacked in magazine racks let you keep favorite stories close at hand.

Wall-mounted clips, cans, and bulletin boards subtly encourage organization and leave room on the desktop for books and papers.

Toy bins, affixed to the inside of cupboard doors, are easily accessed by kids.

Storage bins below the coffee table hold throws, remotes, and other TV-watching essentials.

The fabric sleeve draped over the sofa arm is an easy-to-sew remote-control holder.

Color Palette

To create a color palette for storage, think large to small, and use the palest color as a backdrop. White is a great foundation, as it reflects lots of light and harmonizes with most other hues. Add color with furnishings, or keep them neutral and play with a few bold accent pieces. Sage and wheat are perfect hues for a family room; together, they make things look calm and quiet while subtly keeping storage color-coded and organized.

Room Plan

Divided into three zones – a central entertainment area flanked by areas for work and play – this family room makes the most of square footage and offers ample space for simultaneous activities. The wall of built-in storage balances the need to keep items close at hand with the desire to keep the room neat. The central panel of closed media storage conceals wires (making the room safer for children) and keeps electronics out of sight when they are not in use. Boxes with easy-to-grab handles are stationed near the desk and below the coffee table.

Storage and Care

Toys are best stored where children can reach them. Built-in bookshelves or armoires with custom-built shelving (or with storage baskets on shelves) work well to categorize and display toys and games.

Movies should be organized by subject and stacked label out for easy selection. Store DVDs and videotapes away from extreme temperatures or magnetic toys, to prevent damage or loss of information.

Making Room for Media

Neat, browsable storage is a must for any room devoted to family entertainment. Music, movies, magazines, and games need fitted containers and a smart labeling system. Clever space savers and little conveniences can have a big impact, especially in tight spaces.

Wherever family members gather, their belongings do, too. The coziest room in the house tends to overflow with the very things designed to help us relax – books, CDs, movies, and magazines – and the result can be less than relaxing. To remedy the problem and restore order, employ the basics of storage: contain small items, catalog them with a good labeling system, and take advantage of clear storage.

Containing a collection of media can be approached two ways. Items can be kept behind closed doors, which helps protect them and reduces clutter, or they can be placed in a storage system that becomes a decorative part of the overall room. If you like the sleek look of closed storage, be sure to provide proper ventilation for stereos, DVD players, or any other equipment that generates heat. Graduated and fitted storage, with larger spaces to hold videos and smaller ones to hold CDs, helps keep drawers and closet shelves neat.

If you prefer storage placed in plain view, a mix of practical and unexpected containers is a winning combination. In the shelves shown here, clear plastic file boxes keep music and magazines in stylish order. With a nod to Hollywood, metal film reel canisters are repurposed to store loose photos.

Filed for ease, *left*, CDs are kept within reach and ordered with a simple labeling system. The front CD cases are empty and hold the labels for each cube. **Clear containers**, *right*, can perform organizing wonders, placing things in plain sight without distracting from the decor.

Color Palette

In relatively small rooms where lots of action takes place, a light color on the walls can make the room appear larger and more spacious. However, small rooms offer an opportunity to use bold colors without feeling overwhelmed by the impact of a strong hue. This family media room makes the most of both options: creamy white walls and espresso-colored, streamlined furniture provide a warm backdrop for a high-tech entertainment center. Inside the closet, bright red binders make a graphic, yet practical, statement.

Especially in the family room, the goal of storage is to have things routinely put back in the same spot. A consistent labeling system helps keep small items in order and in place. A cabinet or closet with adjustable shelves, even a small one, is ideal for storing CDs and DVDs as well as photo albums. Use portable labeled caddies so that music and movies are easy to browse and access. This system makes it simple to find just what you want, whether it's energetic music for a busy morning or movies for a lazy Sunday afternoon.

Photogenic filing, *left*, organizes a closet, makes things easy to find, and is easy on the eyes as well. **Identical albums**, *above*, contain favorite photos and decorating inspirations. Sticking to a single style of container is a good choice for an ever-expanding collection.

Storage and Care

CDs/DVDs are damaged most frequently by mishandling and dust and dirt, which cause scratches that can ruin a disc. Keep them in labeled plastic jewel cases or sleeves, but be careful never to write on a disc with anything other than a felt-tip pen.

Magazines are best stored on bookshelves in containers that protect them from dust and hold their form. Label containers for quick access. For long-term storage, store magazines flat in cardboard book boxes (do not pack too tightly as they need air to circulate); store in a cool, dry environment.

Photo albums should be stored in bookshelves or on tabletops for easy viewing. For long-term storage, move photographs to acid-free, photo-specific archival sleeves and into archival boxes. In general, black-and-white photos will last five times longer than color prints, which fade over time.

How to Store Media Collections

Whether music, movies, magazines, or all of the above, media collections tend to be large, and they grow larger every day. To fully enjoy your entertainment, a good portable organization system is essential. Place items in small containers, so they can be pulled from a shelf, browsed through, or carried over to the sofa without creating clutter. Layering items – keeping tall, less-used things in the back of a shelf, favorites in front – also enhances a shelf's functionality. Clear plastic containers let you view contents quickly. Labels point you right where you want to go and make it easy to keep track of a growing collection.

Labeled file folders, *above*, act as subject dividers when slipped between magazines in a simple organizational system. **A drawer devoted to CDs**, *top right*, protects a collection from damage and dust. Use filing accessories from the desktop to keep CDs separated and standing upright with labels showing. **A stack of identical red binders**, *right*, creates an attractive display and maintains visual order while keeping magazine and newspaper clippings neatly filed.

A **galvanized bottle caddy,** *above left,* was borrowed from the kitchen to serve as a tidy spot for remote controls and television listings. **A hand-sewn suede pocket,** *above,* drapes over the arm of a sofa, keeping remote controls out of the way and easy to find. **Metal film reel canisters,** *left,* are repurposed to protect photographs until they can be placed in an album. Stack the reels together to make an eye-catching display. Creative opportunities abound for media storage. Look for unusual containers that echo the entertainment theme of the room.

How to Display Mementos

Treasured photos and lovingly collected artifacts should be proudly displayed. Give mementos pride of place on a wall or shelf — set them high upon a mantel for drama or low on a table for browsing. Your souvenirs may lend themselves to a neat, symmetrical display or they might look best in a casual arrangement. The guidelines for display offer lots of leeway: placing objects in groups of three or five makes an attractive vignette; a single large object or the repetition of many small ones creates visual drama. And don't be shy: use gallery lights to call attention to your display, and choose the best picture frames you can find.

Simple glass vases, *above*, or even covered cake stands make versatile displays. To call attention to small objects or to protect delicate ones from breakage, do as museums do and display them under glass. **Make a wall of family history**, *right*, if genealogy is your passion. Combine old and new photos and mementos, and let them spill onto the furniture. How formal you make the display is up to you. For a museum-quality or formal look, choose identical or closely matched frames. For a more eclectic look, frame each picture or memento in a style to suit its subject or reflect the era from which it dates.

For an easily changed photo gallery, *above left*, borrow a page from your local card shop and mount favorite snapshots on a postcard rack. **Moulding frame ledges**, *left*, offer flexible options for showcasing small collectibles or photos that might get overlooked on a larger shelf or table surface. **First-edition books**, *above*, show their front and back covers in shadow-box frames. Instead of gluing, mount books by lining the back of a frame with a pinboard (covered in acid-neutral paper) and setting the book between rows of T-pins. If your frame has an open front, tie a piece of nylon line loosely around the book.

kitchens

Gathering place and heart of the home, the kitchen has long been the favorite room of the house. Here, storage must meet the expectations of cooks, kids, and visitors alike, and it must do so ingeniously – placing a number of culinary necessities within easy reach and keeping just as many safely put away.

When planning storage for the kitchen, begin with the fixtures and determine the rest from there. The sink, stove, and refrigerator make up the kitchen's work triangle, and good storage should always accommodate this practical layout.

Details are the special ingredients that give kitchen storage its personality; this can be as easy as transferring commonly used items such as dry goods, oils, and teas into decorative canisters or bottles, or as simple as choosing a single color, such as white, for dishes, servingware, and linens.

Make a point of finding storage pieces that are distinctly nontraditional in a kitchen. Even small containers you use to store cutlery or serving utensils can be chosen with individual style and personality in mind. If you have brushed-steel appliances, choose vessels made from the same

Well-planned kitchen storage addresses every need and works for every occasion, from quick snacks and casual dinners to festive holiday entertaining.

Cupboards and open storage should help you in your progression from one station to the next. Keep in mind that simple solutions work best: pots and pans hung over the stove; a tray of cups by the coffeemaker; knives near the prep area.

In a galley kitchen, or a kitchen with an island, closed storage can make a space seem larger and less cluttered by keeping items tucked out of sight. Make the most of the space behind closed storage cabinets by adding adjustable racks or by installing hooks on the backs of cupboard doors. Free up counters or cabinets with the help of a rolling cart with several tiers or by hanging a wrought-iron pot rack from the ceiling.

metal. Or, if you want to draw attention to the patina of your wood cabinetry, enlist wooden bowls for convenient storage of flatware or linen.

Well-planned storage makes room for display, whether it's functional or decorative, and leaves surfaces clear for working. As with any display, there is always strength in numbers. Discover the hidden potential of your china. For a dramatic backdrop to a dining table, create a gallery display of plates or serving platters. Keep spoons and spatulas in a tall vase near the stove. Or, hang a collection of shapely cutting boards over a countertop reserved for food preparation. Everyday objects hold exciting possibilities.

Storing Tableware

Take lessons from an old-fashioned butler's pantry and store your tableware and accessories like a pro. A few tricks of the trade can keep fine china, linens, silver, and crystal in top condition.

There's an art to storing fine tableware. In order to sparkle on the holiday table year after year, your delicate china and silver should be stored with care. Keep fragile china in padded boxes, with felt between each stacked piece to prevent chips and scratches. Guard silverware from tarnish by keeping it in drawers or boxes lined with special tarnish-preventing felt. Store silver away from cotton or velvet, which may contain sulfides that can cause pitting over time. Preserve fine linens by rolling them, unstarched, in acid-free tissue to avoid creasing and discoloration. Wash fragile china and crystal by hand in warm water with mild detergent and dry thoroughly with a lint-free cloth to keep them gleaming for generations.

Well-planned storage, *left*, places heavy items lowest, everyday items at eye level. **Sterling silver and silverplate**, *above*, should be kept away from humidity to prevent tarnish. **Wine glasses**, *right*, should be stored upright to prevent cracking.

Organizing an Eat-in Kitchen

The pleasure of reaching out and finding a pot holder, spatula, or dish towel, just when it is needed, of clearing the table or setting out breakfast with ease, or putting away clean dishes without having to trek across the room: these are the everyday rewards of smart kitchen storage.

Whether it's being used for preparing a large family meal, grabbing breakfast on the go, or as a base for projects and homework, an eat-in kitchen must withstand lots of friendly commotion. In such spaces, keeping things neat is as much a matter of measurements as it is kitchen common sense.

The average kitchen cabinet is about two feet deep, a standard that results in a convenient amount of storage space. Normally, however, the depth of the cabinet makes it difficult to access anything behind the first row of goods, so you may want to opt for more drawers than cupboards if you are renovating or building from scratch. If you have existing cabinets, upgrade them with removable baskets or runner-mounted shelves, which pull out like a drawer. For corner cabinets, try installing a lazy Susan, which will help keep small items from disappearing into the very back.

Whatever size kitchen you have, informally divide its layout to dedicate space to specific activities. It may be second nature to use one part of a kitchen for dining and another for cooking. But by going one step farther and placing the right storage at the right level, you can also keep bill paying and homework neatly separated from cooking and baking.

A wooden trug, *left*, once used to store garden tools, becomes a decorative accent when filled with bottles of vinegar and oil. **Lightweight baskets**, *right*, are practical alternatives to drawers. Equipped for dining and baking needs, they make it easy to transport ingredients and tableware to the countertop.

Built-in storage has many advantages. A central kitchen island can act as a hub of everyday activities, a spacious cabinet, and a dining table, all in one.

The polished surface of this kitchen's limestone center island is apportioned into zones – for food preparation, dining, and serving. Between meals, the same surface serves as a station for homework and hobbies. Underneath, the island harbors baskets, drawers, wide shelves for oversize platters, and a flexible network of closed and open storage.

Abundant and varied storage, *left*, offers clean-lined convenience. If you have the opportunity to start a kitchen from scratch, choose spacious drawers, open cubbies, and compartments such as these to enhance the versatility of a space. **A built-in plate rack**, *above*, keeps frequently used dinnerware at hand and standing safely upright between wooden dowels.

Design Details

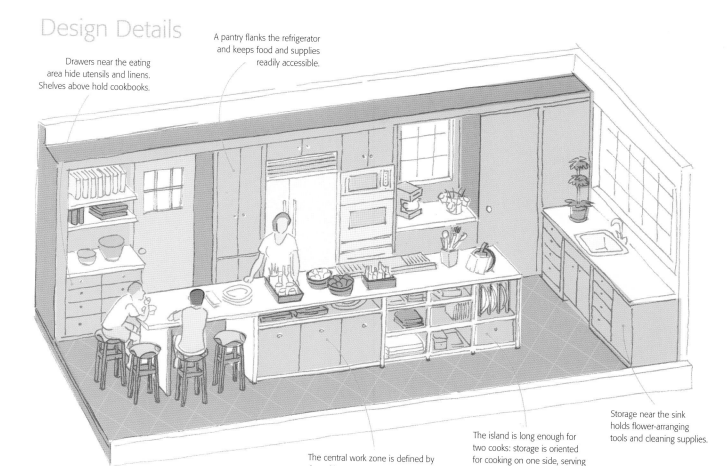

Drawers near the eating area hide utensils and linens. Shelves above hold cookbooks.

A pantry flanks the refrigerator and keeps food and supplies readily accessible.

Storage near the sink holds flower-arranging tools and cleaning supplies.

The central work zone is defined by the refrigerator, range, and oven.

The island is long enough for two cooks: storage is oriented for cooking on one side, serving and table setting on the other.

Color Palette

According to color theory, shades of red and orange stimulate the appetite – a good thing to consider when choosing a palette for an eat-in kitchen. Here, terra-cotta floor tiles and the warm beige of a limestone island blend with honey-colored maple cabinets to create an atmosphere that feels cozy and comforting. An earth-toned color palette has an added advantage – it's easy to keep it looking clean.

Room Plan

In a long, rectangular kitchen, it makes sense to dedicate some counter space to dining as well as cooking and place storage elements so that they bridge the two. For example, set a tray of extra plates between the cooktop and breakfast area. The storage below a kitchen island can also help with zoning. Plan open storage compartments near areas for food preparation, for quick access to cooking oils and other frequently used supplies. Place closed storage near the dining area to hide utensils and other small items and to create a neat, seamless appearance.

Storage and Care

Knives should be stored away from other metal utensils. Store in wood counter or drawer blocks with slats that hold blades secure, or on magnetic bars.

Everyday linens can be stored in shallow drawers or in baskets on open shelves (far enough from the stove so as not to absorb odors or grease). Keep bar towels and dish towels in top drawers near the sink.

How to Create Kitchen Displays

Every kitchen holds wonderful possibilities for creative arrangements, whether by taking advantage of cupboards and countertops or by putting to use narrow spaces above doors, on the sides of cabinets, or along windowsills. When planning displays for your kitchen, choose items that combine style and utility. A collection of bowls and pitchers can be put into service when needed, as can a bouquet, an array of antique utensils, or a stack of handsome cookbooks. When you're creating a display, look at shapes as well as placement. It's always a nice surprise to break up a linear arrangement with a curved object.

Cleverly displayed cookbooks, *top*, take the place of artwork, ready for use. This system employs a fixed rod and a sliding tray that's just the right size to hold books conveniently open and leave countertops clear for cooking. **An antique grill**, *above*, dangles from a knob and serves as a witty clipboard for recipes. **Kitchen chalkboards**, *right*, can stand in for art and offer endless opportunities for organization and fun. Use them to compile shopping lists or display the menu or wine list for a special meal.

Potted plants, *left*, are naturals for fresh, seasonal display in the kitchen. Flowering plants, like these red geraniums, bring vivid color to a pristine white kitchen; the collection of creamware pitchers turns a windowsill into a casual (and functional) still-life arrangement. For the ultimate functional display, cultivate an indoor herb garden to grow ingredients for your favorite recipes. **An antique bottle-drying rack**, *above*, conveniently holds mugs in a niche outfitted for making coffee. Assigning ordinary objects a creative new role often results in an engaging display. You could also stack coffee cups on an étagère or set them inside a domed cake stand to create a witty and practical arrangement for the kitchen.

How to Customize Kitchen Storage

Clever kitchen storage simplifies everyday tasks and helps you work more efficiently. Whether you're planning a new kitchen or working with what you've got, a few small changes can make the most of every inch. Reclaim unused space below cupboards or the stove by installing shallow drawers for cookie sheets and trays. With a little handiwork, the area below a window seat can be transformed into open shelving. Install a slide-out tray or a lazy Susan in deep cabinets to hold cookware and staples. Make the most of narrow wall space or the inside of cupboard doors with hooks or wire racks for hanging serving spoons and large cooking utensils.

Pegboard drawer liners, *above*, are easy to install (most home centers will cut the board to your specifications) and perfect for a myriad of kitchen-organizing tasks. Use them to keep dishes neatly stacked or to prevent strainers, whisks, and other cookware from tangling together. The pegs can be reconfigured in an instant, to customize drawers for new pieces. **Shelves under a window seat**, *right*, are ideal for oversize or unwieldy items like cutting boards and platters. **A marriage of storage and display**, *opposite page*, occupies open shelves in a kitchen island. With deep compartments on the left and shallow shelves on the right, each is suited for different shapes and sizes of dishware.

bedrooms

Bedrooms are often highly personal spaces. The objects we choose to surround us here are an intimate expression of who we are, and the ways we choose to organize them are based on both practical needs and personal style. But one rule trumps all individual preferences: in a space devoted to sleep and relaxation, storage solutions are best kept simple.

With a little planning, bedroom storage can be easily expanded and cleverly concealed. Though capacity is, in part, dictated by the size of closets, even the smallest room can offer large storage table and a place to stow out-of-season clothing; oversized pillows can be piled on the floor in place of an upholstered chair. Scout antique shops and flea markets for shopkeeper's displays and curio cabinets to double as open storage. If you prefer a more unified look, hide belongings from view in hatboxes and baskets.

Display in the bedroom is an even more personal matter, because our private retreats tend to contain our very favorite objects. Open storage can serve the dual purposes of containing and displaying, and can help keep possessions orderly

In a space that's all your own, make storage personal as well as practical. A bedroom offers the chance to arrange things as you truly please.

solutions. The strategic placement of hanging bars and adjustable shelves makes the most of tiny closets. Turn unused corners, recesses, and awkward spaces under eaves into hardworking storage areas to maximize every square foot. Wall-mounted "floating" shelves and stackable storage units provide plentiful possibilities.

A bed, the one essential piece of furniture in the room, can conceal shallow bins and baskets underneath. Beyond that, dressers, side tables, an armoire, or a blanket chest offer many options for stylish hidden storage. Think beyond traditional furniture, especially if you're short on floor space. A stack of vintage suitcases doubles as both a side yet close at hand. You may wish to leave a prized collection of jewelry in full view, arranged artistically on a bureau. For maximum impact, group collectibles together on windowsills and dresser tops. Use your creativity to show off vanity items and framed photographs. Use the bed itself to showcase favorite linens, and mix and match quilts, pillows, and blankets for texture and color. A collection of hats and handbags hung on wall hooks in a pleasing arrangement becomes an eye-catching display. Drape clothing and linens over a dressmaker's form or steamer trunk. The best displays echo the essential nature of a collection, whether it's dramatic, artistic, or playful.

Concealed and Revealed

Bedroom built-ins are nice, but if you're looking for practicality and style, consider flexible furniture that can open wide and snap shut. With your clothes, bedding, books, and accessories tucked tidily out of sight, you can reclaim the bedroom for its true purpose: relaxation.

A serene, uncluttered bedroom is one of life's simple luxuries. With thoughtful use of cupboards and baskets, stowaway carts, and storage that doubles as decor, you can keep belongings concealed from sight and still have plenty of room left for living. Bring in pieces that do more than one thing well: a desk or secretary that opens to reveal a mirror and all the accoutrements of a vanity table; a hamper that can work as a comforter stand; a coffee table that shelters books in a space that would otherwise go to waste. Even if a trundle bed isn't your style, there's no need to let valuable space under the bed go unused. Invest in durable shallow containers for off-season clothes and footwear. For items in regular use, easy-to-construct wooden platforms on wheels provide convenient access to under-bed storage.

If you're in the market for a night table, browse the luggage section of your local thrift store for vintage cloth or leather suitcases. A stack of five or six will give you a handsome tower for a bedside table and as much storage as a whole bureau of drawers. To make short work of loose change and other items that tend to collect on dresser tops, keep a supply of small containers there to catch them.

A classic wood-paneled secretary, *left*, opens to reveal a customized vanity. Mounted with an oval mirror, it also showcases a collection of vintage hand mirrors and brushes. Stacked cake tins provide a tidy place to store cosmetics. A vintage tin cigarette box, *right*, as beautiful as the baubles it holds, displays and safeguards favorite jewelry and accessories.

A light hand with accessories, and a firm one with necessities, is important in order to preserve a feeling of sanctuary in the bedroom. Whatever can't be packed in a drawer or stored in a closet can be placed in the oft-overlooked spaces between floor and furniture. Keep floors free of clutter with plenty of baskets to stow shoes and laundry before they accumulate, and choose furniture with a low profile to ensure clear sight lines across the room.

Roll-out trays, *above*, act as drawers and slide extra linens under the bed and out of sight. They're easily built with ready-made shelves fitted with cabinet handles and casters. **End tables and stacked books**, *right*, form a modular display when draped with a runner. The low-slung "coffee table" does not intrude into the room's visual space the way a tall bookcase would.

EL ARTE DE CARTIER

ECHOS

nonstock

think COLOR GUILD

LIVING WITH ZEN

MODERNISME I MODERNISTES

marchewson

PLACES

INFLUENTIAL INTERIORS Suzanne Trocmé

Bloom Book Li Edelkoort

TADAO ANDO THE COLOURS OF LIGHT RICHARD PARE

FASHION

DREAM of Vases

Design Details

Near the bed, storage is set at every level: a stack of suitcases, a low pair of baskets, and a spacious cabinet.

A wood-paneled desk or secretary can be repurposed as a vanity with multi-use drawers.

Reinvent the blanket chest with two baskets at the foot of the bed.

Storage under a coffee table is neatly hidden from view.

Color Palette

Add interest to a neutral palette by emphasizing a contrast between dark and light. In this bedroom, a color scheme of neutral, stone-colored twill, warm wicker baskets, and deep mahogany is evenly balanced for a repeated play of pale against deep. Like the graphic impact of a black-and-white photo, the contrast of dark woods against light upholstery, and ebonized floors against warm white walls, adds depth to the decor.

Room Plan

In this bedroom, concealed storage contributes to the atmosphere of calm and works with the natural logic of the floor plan. The secretary is conveniently located near the bed and seating areas and makes an informal divider between the small dressing and reading alcoves. Storage that can be closed when not in use is a good way to bring visual organization to a bedroom. Distributing storage evenly throughout a room – below the coffee table, at the nightstands, and along one wall – helps keep belongings close at hand.

Storage and Care

Blankets should be cleaned and dried before folding or rolling and storing away for a season. Best kept in covered chests lined with cedar, heavy blankets should never be stored in plastic, which can trap heat and moisture.

Pillows should always be covered with a washable zippered pillow protector, whether they are stored away in a closet or in use. When necessary, wash in a gentle cycle with an extra rinse and dry thoroughly.

Storage for a Restful Space

The organization of a room can, by its very nature, inspire a sense of order and serenity. In this shared bedroom, an abundance of concealed storage is quietly integrated at every level to keep everyday items out of sight, helping to enhance the open views and soothing style.

As spaces devoted to resting, bedrooms are at their best when they induce a feeling of quiet and calm. A storage dilemma then arises: how do you incorporate all the stuff of life – favorite books, clothing, personal accessories, and collections – without disrupting a relaxing environment? When a sleeping space accommodates the habits of two people, storage must be doubly hardworking.

In any bedroom, the bed is the functional heart of the space. It also harbors one of the most overlooked sources of hidden storage: the space underneath. A tucked-away under-bed storage system keeps clutter neatly out of sight. This room's custom platform bed is actually a configuration of low bookcases covered by a plywood sheet and topped with a mattress. Woven baskets slip into the compartments to keep clothing, reading material, and bedside necessities conveniently hidden but easy to reach.

Solving storage problems reinforces the orderly beauty of a room. Edit your belongings to further reduce visual clutter in the bedroom. Instead of table lamps, install hanging or wall-mounted lights to save space on bedside tables.

Woven baskets, *left*, pull out from a platform bed formed by a framework of low bookcases. The serenity of this bedroom relies on the hardworking storage hidden in plain sight. **A tailored slipcover**, *right*, encloses a bedside table; a pair of pendant lights keep the streamlined cubes free and clear.

Color Palette

The freshness associated with certain shades of green can be used to great advantage in a bedroom. Calling to mind calming images of nature and the clean scent of spring, the yellow green used here adds to the overall feeling of tranquility. Paler shades of green envelop the rest of the room. The amber tones of the maple bed frame and the bleached walnut floors enhance the natural palette, while latte-colored bedding and linen slipcovers add subtle accents throughout.

Dividing a bedroom into comfortable zones for sleeping and relaxing naturally makes it more organized. This bedroom for two includes a peaceful sitting area with dramatic views of the countryside. The easy-living space is furnished with only a few practical but generous foundation pieces – a luxurious bed and a pair of chaise longues, both supplied with extra pillows for lounging or reading.

Storage and Care

Duvets, whether they are filled with down or a hypoallergenic fill, should always be kept in a washable cover. When needed, have duvets laundered or dry-cleaned professionally. For space-saving long-term storage, fold your duvet into a narrow strip, roll up, and secure with a wide ribbon.

Slipcovers should be kept out of direct sunlight to prevent fading. Store away for the season when clean and thoroughly dry. Slipcovers can usually be spot-cleaned with a towel dampened with club soda, but be sure to launder according to instructions.

Basket storage should offer enough room to keep woven baskets from being bent or crushed. Stored on a shelf or in a cubby, a full basket should have enough room to slide out easily. To make baskets last, keep them away from heat and dampness and don't overfill them.

Clever storage planning, *left*, leaves this bedroom's sitting area wide open for relaxation. The stack of pillows forms a soft sculpture – and extra seating. **A portable wooden tray**, *above*, holds a still life of sensory treats: incense, music, an aromatherapy candle, a journal, and a ceramic stone engraved with the word "calm."

How to Store Linens and Pillows

Proper storage for linens follows much the same guidelines as proper storage for clothing. First, arrange things so there's enough room for air to circulate, allowing fabric to breathe. Cover items in long-term storage to protect them from dust, and choose fabric or paper storage cases rather than plastic options. Place everyday items within reach; stow heavy blankets and coverlets down low, and extra pillows up high. If you have a blanket chest, you'll be able to see more of the contents if you roll blankets rather than stacking them in layers. Line drawers or cupboards with white, acid-free tissue before storing delicate or antique linens.

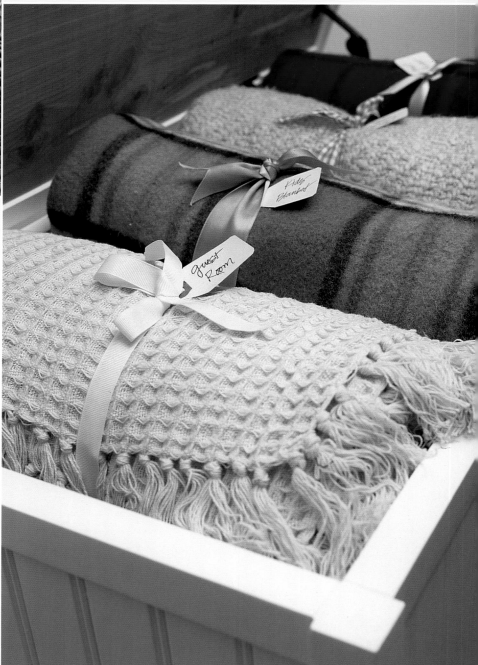

Label your linens, *above*, with clothespins and tags to keep linen chests tidy. When sheets are labeled as flat, fitted, or European, you won't have to rummage to find the size you want. Pegs and labels can be kept right in the linen chest, awaiting clean sets of sheets. If you prefer closet storage, label shelves to keep things organized and to prevent different-size linens from being mixed together in a stack. **Roll extra blankets**, *right*, and secure them with ribbon ties before storing them in a cedar chest. This approach, as decorative as it is useful, makes it easy to find just what you are looking for.

Linen closet tradition, *left*, suggests sorting sets of linens by size – twin, full, queen – and then grouping them by bedroom – children's room, guest room, master bedroom, and so on. If space is at a premium, store table linens elsewhere, so the linen closet isn't packed too tightly. Keep stacks shallow so that folded items can be easily removed or replaced. Everyday sheet sets should be low enough to grasp without reaching above your shoulders or below your waist. To ensure even wear, rotate linens by placing clean laundry at the bottom of the stack and removing fresh supplies from the top. **Fabric packets**, *below*, can be filled with lavender or cedar and tucked into drawers or closets for fresh scent.

closets

Closets offer an excellent opportunity to organize the stuff of life. That may sound like a tall order, but rearranging a closet is really just a matter of breaking down the project into stages. Once you get started, you'll discover space you didn't know you had.

First, pare down your belongings to eliminate things you don't need. The fewer items you have to worry about, the easier the job of organizing them will be. Donate the clothes that no longer fit you or your lifestyle to the thrift shop; old books, CDs, and movies to your local library; toys and games to a daycare center. Purge your china cupboard and linen closet, too. Pass on anything that languishes unused and is not dear to you, beautiful, or useful. Consider whether some items could be better stored elsewhere in the house – under the bed, or in the attic or basement.

again into hangables, stackables, odd sizes, and articles that can be folded, rolled, or collected in smaller containers. Set up a flexible storage plan that accommodates your wardrobe, anticipates seasonal changes, and fits the way you dress.

Make a list of the closet accessories that are most likely to help you maintain order. Are extra handbags or spare linens easier to reach on shelves or hung up on a rod? Does the space or your habits call for a hanging shoe bag or a stack of shoeboxes? Note how many hangers you'll need to keep all of your clothes stored properly.

Having an orderly closet is the next best thing to having a personal valet. Both help you look your best, and both make it easier to triumph over chaos.

The next step is to take everything out of the closet and make an inventory. Separate household items into groups for upstairs and downstairs, categorized by room. Once it's all divided into stacks, organize things by size and shape and return to each closet accordingly. For a clothes closet or wardrobe, divide clothing into daily or occasional use, seasonal or year-round. Then sort

When it comes to hangers, shapes count as much as quantity, so make sure you have wooden hangers for jackets, clip hangers for pants and skirts, and padded hangers for delicate items.

When it's time to put it all back, review your new closet setup. If it still seems crowded, can more shelves be added, or can they be further divided to better organize stacked clothing? Above all, be realistic. Think of how you're going to get to something when you need it, and how often that's likely to be. Getting organized is meant to make your life run more smoothly. If you design your closet to mirror your priorities, everything is bound to fall right into place.

Planning a Walk-in Closet

A successful closet makeover begins with an inventory. Take stock of your wardrobe and dressing habits and customize storage to fit the way you live. This spacious walk-in dressing room offers lessons in planning for closets of all sizes and wardrobes of all shapes.

Sustainable order and near-instant accessibility is the necessary combination for a successful closet, whether it's a spacious dressing room or a tiny enclosure under the stairs. With intelligent space planning, the conveniences of a fully customized walk-in closet can be adapted to fit any closet.

Good closet management begins with the hanger. A hanger should be chosen with an eye toward supporting the weight of a garment while maintaining the garment's shape. Padded hangers and ones with notches or nonslip surfaces are well suited to lightweight clothing, especially items made of slippery fabrics or those with straps. Wooden hangers are best for heavier garments like robes, jackets, and coats. Because they will stretch out, knits should never be hung. Instead, fold them in drawers or containers, with cedar blocks added to discourage moths.

In this well-appointed closet, a clever configuration of hanging bars, chests of drawers, and open shelving provides space to hang or store any item according to season, style, and frequency of use. A dresser built into the middle of the space becomes a functional island, its bottom section a chest of roomy drawers, its top surface a sleek vanity.

Hangers keyed to fabric and style, *left*, keep a closet full of clothing in prime condition. **Floor-to-ceiling shelves**, *right*, allow for open storage of shoes and closed-box storage identified by content labels. Wooden boxes make it easy to select from an array of rolled neckties or a stack of sweaters.

No matter what size your closet, begin by dividing it into sections, and install multiple closet rods to maximize space. Place the most frequently worn items in the center of the space, at eye level. Dedicate the upper sections for infrequently used or off-season items. Hang short garments together in two rows; use the lower hanger bar for skirts and pants, and the upper bar for blouses, shirts, and jackets.

Designed to suit the way you live every day, an organized closet is a thing of great beauty.

If space allows, bring in a small, narrow dresser for closed storage. For seasonal storage, use zippered garment bags for hanging items, and lidded boxes for folded, flat storage. In smaller closets, use a pocket shoe organizer to hold small accessories. Always clean garments before putting them away for a season. Remove dry-cleaner bags before hanging clothes, and sandwich tissue paper between layers of folded fabric.

A clothing repair station, *left*, holds sewing notions. Glass jars let you see the contents at a glance. **A center island**, *right*, serves as a vanity table for dressing while offering deep drawers for storage. Shaded table lamps cast flattering light for dressing and trying on jewelry.

Design Details

Clothing worn during the work week is kept in the center for easy access.

Clothes are organized by length and style: dresses in one section, jackets and skirts in the next.

Less frequently worn items such as gowns can be stored in garment bags and hung in a back corner.

A hamper is set within the dressing area to keep laundry off the floor.

An island is a convenient feature for a walk-in closet. It provides extra storage or surface space.

Color Palette

Though they're often too small to fit more than one hue, closets and dressing rooms are the perfect places in which to use a favorite color that's not ideal for a whole room. In this case, white walls and shelving offer a clean, unbiased backdrop to a spacious walk-in closet. Colorful accents of robin's-egg blue add a touch of whimsy, while blond beech wood helps identify storage for accessories.

Room Plan

The well-designed closet includes plenty of clever extras: built-in shelf dividers, cubbies in a range of widths and depths, dedicated shelves for luggage and shoe storage, and a slide-out panel or deep countertop for folding clothes. Drawers should include dividing inserts, and hardware should be effortless to operate. If there's space, include a small bureau with drawers in graduated sizes — small and shallow for jewelry or lingerie, deeper for grooming supplies and clothes. A mirrored panel hung on the door turns the closet into a dressing room.

Storage and Care

Wool sweaters should be dry-cleaned before storing for the season. Place in canvas or fabric bags, and store in cedar chests or in storage boxes with cedar blocks, in a cool, dry space away from direct sunlight.

Shoes are best kept in acid-free boxes or on shoe racks. Use cedar wood trees in leather shoes. For cloth shoes, fill the toe with tissue paper to hold the shape. Always let shoes air out before storing.

A vintage chocolate container, *above*, makes the perfect home for hats or accessories (paper and cardboard allow air in but filter dust out). Contrary to popular belief, sheathing clothing in plastic is not the best long-term storage method. Fabric fibers break down when deprived of oxygen.

An antique dressmaker's form, *right*, brings storage into the room and turns an embroidered silk ensemble into a display. If you store clothing out in the open, place it away from strong sunlight, which can damage the fabric.

How to Store Clothing

Clothes are like their owners: happiest when given enough space, rumpled when crowded together. Whether folded in a drawer or hanging in a closet, clothing benefits from free circulation of air and plenty of elbow room. Too many pieces squeezed into too small an area also makes getting to individual garments harder than it needs to be. Take stock of what you most need in your primary closet, and move seldom-worn pieces to other storage. To allow more air to circulate, replace closet doors or armoire doors with scrims of linen or cotton fabric – a trick that creates an illusion of greater space as well.

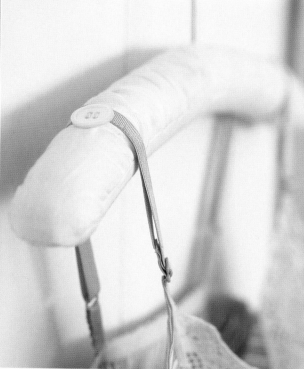

Wooden caddies, *left,* present a selection of rolled neckties for easy access. Neckties can be stored loosely rolled or hung up, depending on your closet configuration. **A glass jar of cedar balls,** *top,* imparts a fresh fragrance and protects against moths. A bottle of cedar oil stands nearby, for replenishing the scent. **Garments with thin straps,** *above,* no longer slip to the floor when anchored by buttons sewn to a padded hanger.

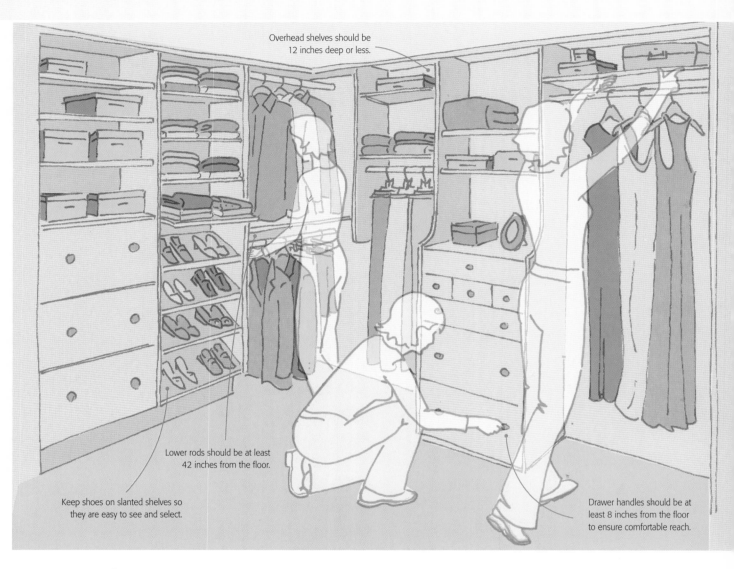

Overhead shelves should be 12 inches deep or less.

Lower rods should be at least 42 inches from the floor.

Keep shoes on slanted shelves so they are easy to see and select.

Drawer handles should be at least 8 inches from the floor to ensure comfortable reach.

Customizing a Closet

Planning a closet begins with a wardrobe assessment. First, sort your clothing and pare it down to a manageable minimum. Then plan each segment of the closet for specific types of clothing – double-hung closet rods for shirts, skirts, and slacks; high closet rods for dresses and coats; open shelves for sweaters, accessories, and luggage. Last, add the extras: shoe racks, accessory drawers, and mirrors.

Fabrics need air to keep them looking their best. Stacking rods in tiers is the best way to add more space to a closet (so air can circulate freely). Place the lowest closet rod 42 inches from the floor – anything lower is awkward to reach and may not provide enough clearance for long skirts and pants. Place the upper rod at least 36 inches above the lower rod. Install all rods 12 inches from the back of the closet to allow 2 inches of clearance for hangers.

Using these guidelines and our chart of specific measurements for each type of clothing (at right), you'll have a better idea of how much space to allot for double-hung rods, how much you need for long garments like dresses and coats, and how much shelf space you need for sweaters, knits, and shoes. Finally, be generous in your assessments in order to keep clothing from being crushed and to make room for new additions to your wardrobe.

and organizing its contents to keep your clothing looking its best

Dress Shirts

Hang shirts on upper closet rods in the middle of the closet.

Width Shirts occupy 1 to 2 inches of rod space. Six hanging shirts take up approximately 1 linear foot.

Length Allow at least 40 inches for hanging men's shirts and at least 38 for women's shirts and blouses.

Dresses

Hang dresses in their own section, arranged from shortest length to longest.

Width Plan on 1 to 3 inches of rod space for each dress, approximately four dresses per linear foot.

Length Allow at least 43 inches of hanging space, 60 inches for formal wear.

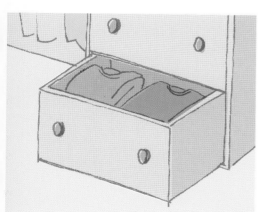

Sweaters

All sweaters should be folded. For easy access, place them on pull-out trays between waist and shoulder height.

Width Allow at least 12 inches of shelf space per stack.

Height Thick sweaters are 2 to 6 inches high when folded. Keep stacks to four or fewer sweaters.

Suits

Hang suits as a unit, or with jackets on the top rod and skirts or pants below.

Width Each jacket takes up 3 to 4 inches. Allow 2 inches for pants or skirts.

Length On average, skirts need 23 to 43 inches; suit pants require 40 to 60 inches; jackets need 27 to 40 inches.

Casual Shirts

T-shirts should be folded, stacked, and stored in drawers or on open shelves.

Width T-shirts require 9 to 10 inches of shelf space; casual button-down cotton shirts require 9 inches.

Depth A stack of six T-shirts requires a drawer at least 6 inches deep to ensure adequate clearance.

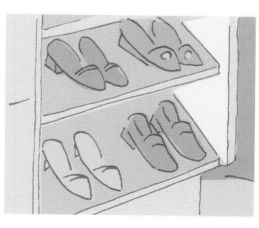

Shoes

Store low on open shelves for visibility and easy access.

Width Allow 7 to 8 inches of shelf space per pair for women's shoes, 8 to 10 inches for men's shoes.

Depth Plan on 12 to 14 inches for shoe shelves. It's difficult to see into shelves deeper than 16 inches.

How to Store Accessories

Sometimes it's the little things that seem hardest to contain – items that peek out of drawers or slide to the closet floor when you're busy looking for something else. When it comes to storing accessories, it's largely a matter of what's in view. Ideally, the better you can see your accessories, the more you will want to use them. You should be able to locate the right scarf or find the perfect shoe in a single glance. Accessories should be arranged to let your gaze fall on things unexpectedly, encouraging you to browse. Think of your accessory storage as your own little shop window – with treasures on display, awaiting discovery.

Laboratory glass, *above*, is perfectly sized for keeping jewelry from tangling or getting lost or scratched. Made of tempered glass, these containers are durable and make it easy to find just what you are looking for in a jewelry box or drawer. **Reinvent the shoebox**, *right*, with plain, reinforced versions. For quick identification, label the boxes with ribbons color-coded to match the shoes within. Put dress shoes on the bottom row and everyday shoes stacked on top.

Rain boots and work boots, *left*, can be tucked out of the way in the cubbies of a mudroom bench. Line boot storage with a galvanized tray or rubber mat to collect rain or melted snow from soggy footwear and contain puddles. **A bath towel rod**, *above*, fitted with snap-open rings becomes a handy system for storing handbags where they won't get crushed, and placing them in plain view and within reach. To keep bags in shape, stuff them with tissue or kraft paper and leave them open to ensure air circulation.

Three Ways to Organize a Drawer

Busy mornings run more smoothly when accessories are organized and in reach. Customize drawers to their contents and you'll not only save space, you'll have a system so intelligently planned that it's nearly impossible to put things back in the wrong place.

Fit a drawer for jewelry storage by adding clear boxes and fabric- or leather-lined trays to create removable compartments. Stackable, open dividers let you see what you have at a glance. In jewelry drawers, smaller and more variously sized compartments equal a neater and more organized collection.

The rule is also "divide and conquer" when storing socks and men's accessories. Stow one pair of socks in each segment of a flexible drawer divider and you'll never find yourself rummaging through the bureau again. Save room in the front of the drawer for a tray to catch collar stays, cufflinks, and other items.

The "filing cabinet approach" works best for lingerie drawers. Sort your delicates by style and color, and place like with like. Set everyday lingerie items in the front, where they'll be easy to grab when dressing.

Store fragile pieces singly, and only place one or two items in each compartment.

Place a divided tray for small accessories in front, where you can see it.

Line wooden drawers to keep lingerie and other delicates from snagging.

the best storage for your wardrobe

Item	Hanger Style	How to Choose	Best Location	Long-Term Storage
Shirts		Look for smooth wood with a slight curve to the arms. The hanger's shape should follow the natural slope of shoulders.	Shirts that are in everyday use should be stored at eye level, in the middle of the closet, above trousers or skirts.	Button all the buttons to keep a hanging shirt crisp. Don't store in plastic garment bags, which can cause cloth to yellow.
Trousers		Clamp hangers allow trousers to hang straight down, which will help them retain a crease. Clamp trousers at the hemline or cuff.	Place dress trousers all together, arranged by color and fabric weight, adjacent to the shirts with which they are matched.	Group in garment bags by fabric. Silk, wool, and leather need extra protection from insects. Cotton and linen need less care.
Casual Pants		Use a wooden hanger with a sturdy rod. Jeans, corduroys, and khaki pants do better folded and stacked on a shelf.	Use a low closet rod if the pants are hung. Otherwise, lay twills and khakis flat on shelves; use stacked cubbies for jeans.	Wood is acidic and can deteriorate fabric, so line wooden shelves with muslin if you're storing clothing for more than six months.
Dresses		The rounded shape of a padded hanger protects the thin straps of formal dresses and keeps delicate dress fabrics from denting.	Hang short dresses together and long with long, on upper closet rods. Dedicate easy-access space to everyday dresses.	Remove dry-cleaner bags (plastic traps moisture in the fabric's fiber). Hang in canvas or muslin garment bags or wrap in a clean sheet.
Skirts		Use hangers with moveable clips that fit various waistbands and fabrics. Prevent clip marks by padding with folded tissue.	Place on lower-tier rods, below matching shirts and blouses. Arrange by color and length – shortest to longest.	To protect the shapes of bias-cut and A-line skirts, store them folded. Hang delicate items by their straps on padded hangers.
Suits		Seek smooth wooden hangers with a bar to hold pants. Wide, contoured shoulders help jacket shoulders keep their shape.	Place on upper-tier rods, in the middle of the closet if worn daily. Place in less accessible areas if worn infrequently.	The ideal storage climate is cool, dark, and dry. Loosely stuff sleeves with acid-free tissue and store in hanging fabric bags.
Coats		Coats require sturdy hangers that can support their weight. Look for hangers with wide, curved arms to keep shoulder seams intact.	Store bulky coats separately from primary garment storage. Avoid packing coats tightly – let air circulate around them.	Lay heavy coats flat in a storage box. Otherwise, cloth garment bags are essential for keeping leather and fur ventilated.
Sweaters		Keep sweaters folded flat. In a pinch, they can be folded with acid-free tissue and draped on the bar of a wooden hanger.	Place in stacked cubbies, hanging canvas bags, or on open shelves. Sort by color, season, and sleeve length; limit stacks to four.	Fold wool, cashmere, and silk sweaters in acid-free tissue and store in canvas or muslin boxes, with cedar blocks to repel moths.

bathrooms

When it comes to finding bathroom storage, appearances can often be deceiving. Although you can make a bathroom appear large, it's usually the smallest room in the house. And while things that are stored in the bath may seem small, they often require twice the space you had planned. In the bathroom, the sheer number of items needing storage is likely to be greater than in any room but the kitchen. Beauty products and shaving supplies, gels and potions, towels and hair dryers are just a few of the items that make up the list.

enough counter space for each person. A family bathroom calls for a flexible storage solution that addresses the needs of adults and kids alike.

Always plan from the inside out. Apart from making the most of the space available, choose storage that's fitted to its contents and convenient to your habits. Clear, open storage puts attractive bath supplies both in view and on display. Closed storage – whether in drawers, lidded bins, wall-hung or under-counter cabinets – presents a neat impression and protects contents from moisture. Keeping some items in closed storage also ensures

Simple storage elements can make a room shine. A trim cabinet, a tidy row of shelves – it only takes a few details to add convenience and comfort to the bath.

In addition to being stocked full of supplies, most bathrooms are also shared spaces. They must serve users of many shapes and sizes and balance the practical needs of the household with the occasional needs of guests. It's a lot to ask of one little room, which is why a bathroom's storage system should be particularly well thought out.

Start by determining who uses the room most, its busiest time of day, and how it's primarily used. A bathroom where lots of showers are taken is going to be more humid than a powder room off the front hall, so it will require more attention in protecting items from dampness. For a busy couple's master bathroom, there should be

that favorite pieces left out to be admired don't have to compete for attention with their less beautiful relations. Decanting toiletries into amber or cobalt blue glass containers offers both practicality and beauty; dark, colored glass has been traditionally used to protect potions from sunlight, which helps to preserve their potency.

Whatever your personal style and whatever the architectural limits of your space, remember that in designing bathroom storage, the ultimate goal is to achieve an overall feeling of calm. Storage can be decorative or invisible, but above all, it should create a sense of order and make the bath a place of sanctuary to all who use it.

A Master Plan for a Master Bath

A his-and-her bathroom is zoned with double sinks, plenty of space for privacy, and lots of built-in storage. Customized cabinets paired with handsome containers double the storage capacity and minimize clutter to create a refined bath with enough room for two.

No matter how spacious a master bath, put two people in it at the same time and it can feel cramped. How do you design an environment for two that's as well suited to morning rush hour as it is to unwinding at the end of the day? The solution is a design that allows equal time in front of the mirror, equal access to the sink and shower, and equal amounts of storage space.

This master bath serves up all of the above in a luxurious combination of mahogany and limestone. Double sinks set into a limestone countertop define "his" and "hers" zones that are reinforced by the subdivision of drawers and cabinets beneath. Twin medicine cabinets, recessed into the walls at both ends of the vanity, read as square white-on-white panels beneath square light fixtures. An uninterrupted wall of mirror visually opens up the narrow room to create a greater sense of space.

Perhaps the room's most dramatic innovation is its subdivision into discrete zones. A partial wall separates the sink area from the shower/toilet alcove, ensuring a degree of privacy and visually balancing the room's elongated shape.

An even arrangement of built-in storage, *left*, in the mahogany vanity and discreet wall cabinets, creates enough space for both users to store their toiletries and leaves counter space to display attractive bath supplies. **A recessed shelf**, *right*, over the toilet makes art of everyday items.

The uncluttered look of this master bath owes much of its serenity to the thoughtful storage ideas at work behind the scenes. Multiple built-in compartments provide generous and easily accessed storage for grooming aids, cosmetics, and bath supplies. Each drawer and cupboard is fitted with custom-sized containers to keep smaller items organized and easy to locate during a busy morning.

An artful blend of clean lines and gently curved fittings is highlighted by an absence of clutter.

In place of standard faucets, mirror-mounted fittings appear to float above the basins, freeing up counter space for displays of his, her, and shared bath essentials. The subtle contrast between the rectangular lines of the room's cabinets and the curves of a collection of glass accessories presents a unified front.

Clear glass containers, *left*, compose a still life of toiletries arranged in plain view, while the necessary clutter of daily life is "filed" out of sight. **A mismatched collection of containers**, *right*, makes drawer organization simple: lipsticks stashed in cardboard takeout boxes, bobby pins and hair accessories in a recycled tin, tweezers and clippers in a wooden soap box.

Design Details

Shelves turn a narrow area above the toilet into storage space for towels and supplies.

Recessed medicine cabinets with touch latches blend into the wall for seamless storage.

Shower and tub are back to back, allowing the space to be shared without feeling crowded.

Mirror-mounted faucets leave counters clear for display and make countertops easier to clean.

Color Palette

A neutral combination of creamy white and espresso brown with stainless steel accents complements this sophisticated master bath. Warm white on the walls, floors, and counters sets a uniform backdrop for the stained mahogany cabinets and dark wood trim throughout the room. Sleek stainless steel fittings and hardware are combined with clear glass accessories to reflect light and create a contemporary atmosphere.

Room Plan

Separating the bathroom's showering and bathing areas allows for more than one user at a time. Storage is separated as well, with storage shelves recessed into the wall behind the toilet and a vanity with cabinets and drawers across from the tub. Each space addresses individual needs. The shelves place fresh towels, extra soaps, and shampoo within easy reach of the shower. The vanity's built-in cabinets and drawers are as accessible to the tub as they are to the sinks. The generous countertop holds useful displays that help define his-and-hers areas.

Storage and Care

Soaps can quickly dry out or disintegrate if stored improperly. A soap dish with a built-in drain is best for keeping soaps near a sink. For a scented display, unwrap soaps and place them in open containers.

Grooming accessories may be kept in fitted containers. Preserve the points of tweezers and scissors by keeping them in individual cases. Store metal items as far from the shower as possible.

Storage Solutions for a Family Bath

From hurried mornings to busy bathtimes, a family bathroom is in constant need of efficient storage. One way to provide plenty is to divide and conquer: a two-sided built-in cabinet supplies enough storage space for everyone in the household, from tall to small.

When a bathroom is used by the whole family, you need to keep things organized and clear of the splash zone. More than anything else, storage in the family bath must be flexible, with everything from bath supplies to flotillas of toys neatly in place. And it must provide storage areas that are easy for children to reach, and some that are just for adults. Keeping floor space free and clear of clutter is also on the list. In the compact space of the bath, finding storage that satisfies all these requirements can be a challenge.

A built-in divider offers one practical solution. While vanities and cabinets provide plentiful storage, they also take up valuable floor space. By building up instead of out, you create storage out of thin air and leave more room for foot traffic. Dividers also help to carve out zones for bathing and grooming, allowing users to share the space more easily. This efficient bathroom is a good example. The cabinet becomes a partial room divider, with storage on both sides that makes the most of each space. The tub side of the room is kid friendly, with low hooks for towels and a step stool for small bathers. The sink area is outfitted for adults. Both sides neatly store every essential a busy family might need.

Waterproof plastic bins, *left*, hold toys and bath supplies at the ready. Repurposed trashcans or beach pails can also keep wet items organized. **Double the storage space**, *right*, with back-to-back cabinet compartments. This unit places shallow storage for cosmetics on one side, deep shelves for towels on the other. The lower half of the cabinet hides a laundry chute.

Color Palette

Everyone's favorite color, blue, paired with a pure white makes a classic combination that is perfect for a family bath. Here, a wealth of white — from the ivory wainscoting to the porcelain fixtures — reflects light and provides a clean backdrop. High on the walls and on the ceiling, a coat of light blue paint, with its suggestion of calm seas and clear skies, is the ideal color for a busy bathroom. A plentiful supply of towels adds subtle accents of warm taupe and a range of fresh hues.

While closed cabinets are great for putting your bath's best face forward, open storage is handy for keeping just what's needed readily accessible. The arrangement shown here offers the best of both worlds – hiding cosmetics from passersby on the side of the bathroom facing the hallway and placing storage within view on the tub side of things. If a built-in won't work for your space, you can create a similar layout with a pair of small bookcases or stacked storage cubes (with some openings facing one side of the room, some facing the opposite side).

Storage and Care

Bath towels can be stored on hanging wall racks, shelves, glass-fronted cabinets, or in linen closets. Keep bath towels separate from hand towels by folding one and storing the other rolled up.

Tub toys should be washed and dried thoroughly before storing. Keep in woven wire baskets or vented plastic bins on the tub's edge, on an open shelf, or within easy carrying distance. Open storage containers will allow air to circulate and help to prevent mildew.

Artwork in the bath should be protected from the room's high humidity and kept well away from faucets and fixtures. Use acid-free mats and conservation-style framing; for especially steamy baths, have art professionally encapsulated in an airtight frame or shadow box.

Out of the splash zone, *left*, but within reach, hand towels are rolled and easy to identify among folded bath towels. **A repurposed curtain rod**, *above*, holds magazines and extra paper rolls. Lightweight and waterproof, a trio of translucent plastic bins is an ideal way to keep kids' and parents' bath supplies separate.

Storage on Display

Part traditional bath, part spa, and all indulgence: a welcoming master bath provides rest from the world and a place to relax together. Aim for domestic harmony in an easy-maintenance setting. Choose spa-inspired luxuries and add stylish touches of your own.

At the end of a long day, some couples find that the most relaxing place to be isn't the living room – it's the home spa formerly known as the master bathroom. More haven than grooming center, it's a place for calm relaxation and long soaks, for small talk and big talk, for companionable silence and for catching up. Like a good marriage, storage in a shared bath acknowledges personal preferences and individual taste, yet manages to harmonize them gracefully. It supplies plenty of space for bathing indulgences as well as plenty of drawers and shelf space for each partner – all anchored by a soothing color palette, whether cool hues, warm tones, or the natural shades of wood and stone. In a shared bath, "extras" become essentials: added shelving tucked into corners or under windows; a pair of recessed medicine cabinets; baskets to hold more towels.

In this shared bath, an oversize tub occupies center stage, and alcoves designed for his-and-her relaxation are built into the large room. One corner is designated for beauty treatments while the opposite corner is dedicated to grooming and shaving. The layout employs custom-built storage to accommodate each user's spa essentials.

A spa tray, *left*, borrows elegant servingware from the dining room, including a compote and crystal vases. Storing supplies on trays makes them easy to transport. A well-stocked "beauty bar," *right*, offers a personal menu of bath and spa amenities, from incense sticks and scented candles to relaxing music.

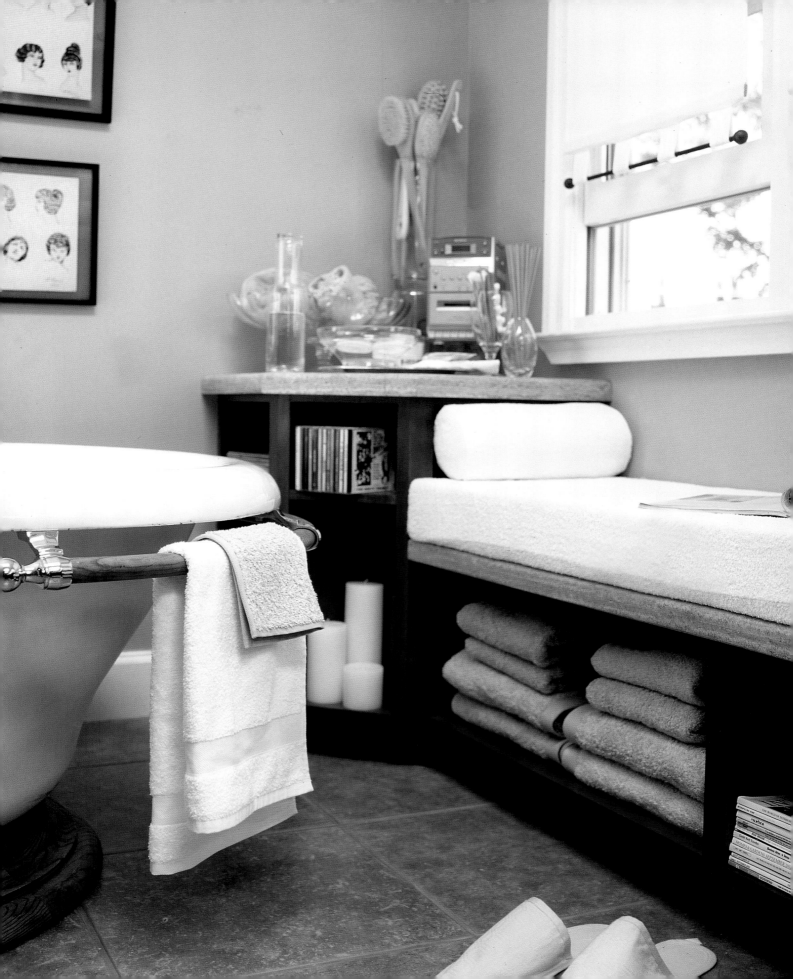

The greatest asset for a shared bath is an abundance of space. But even if you don't have an excess of square footage, you can still make the most of the space you have by arranging cabinets and countertops to cater to your routine. Add drawer and cabinet dividers to increase useful storage space and to free the counter for favorite amenities. Bath supplies can double as decoration when arranged in whimsical containers.

Generous built-in storage and wide expanses of counter space guarantee plenty of room for two.

The spacious storage in this bath includes discrete zones for daily rituals and areas for more leisurely sojourns. Each person is assigned a designated vanity area, which adds an element of privacy and prevents counter space confusion. Gleaming touches such as mirrored trays, a silver pedestal, and an abundance of brushes, make grooming supplies decorative accessories and enhance the sense of a pampering retreat.

"Madame's" side of the vanity, *left*, features her array of mirrored trays and a domed cake stand filled with powder puffs. "Monsieur's" grooming station, *right*, is a handsome study in silver, pewter, and chrome.

A built-in window bench makes a cozy place to finish a last chapter of a book, keep a bath-taking mate company, or enjoy a sunny seat for a manicure and pedicure. The generous supply of fresh towels tucked underneath evokes the atmosphere of a luxurious spa. A similar effect could be achieved with a freestanding chaise longue, daybed, or chair and ottoman combination.

A bench upholstered in white terry is a simple way to turn an ordinary bath into a home spa.

Built-in cabinetry of alder stained with a cherry finish has both a timeless look and a pragmatic design. The deep drawers are fitted with customized partitions to make the most of their capacity. Antique mirrored trays add flexibility to the room's storage: they can be easily transported to the tub or to seating areas when needed. A few well-placed details, such as sculpted chrome fittings and polished wood, can help make storage as much of a luxury as it is a convenience.

A reproduction vintage tub, antique-style chrome fittings, and a palette of rich materials give this room the feel of a day spa. Roller shades control light and privacy, and wall-mounted ring hooks keep towels handy.

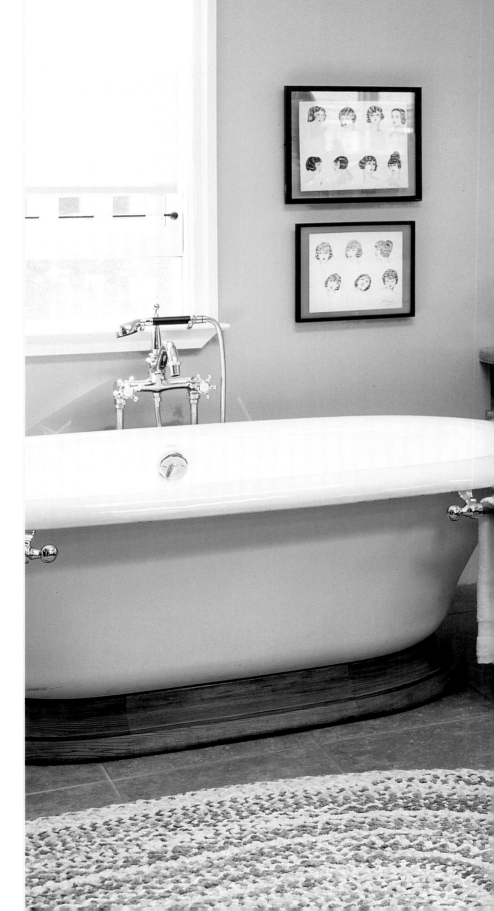

Color Palette

This spa-style master bath combines rich materials and neutral colors for a soothing, luxurious effect. An elegant shade of taupe on the walls sets the stage for a palette of varying shades of brown. The mottled yellow limestone used for the counters, and the warm brown stone used for floor tiles, add depth and texture to the room. Cabinets made of cherry-stained alder reveal a smooth grain that stands out in contrast to the white terry cloth upholstery and trim on the walls.

The meditative spell of a spa-bath can easily be broken by disorder. Although you need a bathroom that accommodates the quick before-work brush up, you don't want the accoutrements of your daily routine to upset the bath's soothing atmosphere. Supply stylish, even luxurious, containers to help corral small, loose items. In this tidy bathroom, the whimsical addition of glass cake stands and a compact overnight case add storage capacity for extra soaps and grooming supplies.

A built-in bench, *left*, features a cubby for magazines, books, towels, and bath supplies. Period accessories add a dignified touch and enrich the look of this bath. **A vintage overnight case**, *above*, is fitted with strawberry-container dividers. It makes a perfect stay-put storage locker for extra cosmetics or items used only now and then.

Storage and Care

Fresh towels can be hung on hooks and heated towel bars within easy reach from the shower or tub. They can also be folded in a linen closet or shelf, but be sure to stack them loosely so they retain their just-washed fluffiness. Tucking dryer sheets or sachets between stacks can help to keep towels smelling fresh and fragrant.

Cosmetics should be stored away from light, humidity, and extreme temperatures. Scent compounds in perfumes and colognes deteriorate in heat and sunlight. Watch expiration dates, too. Most creams have a shelf life of one year; mascara should be replaced every six months.

Shaving supplies should be stored in a cool, dry place. Keep cans of shaving cream away from extreme heat. Razors and scissors should be dried before storing and kept in sheaths for safety.

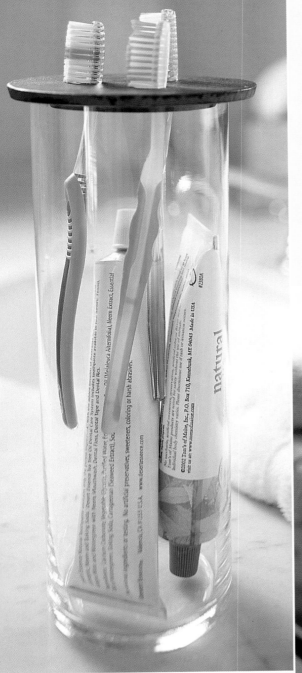

How to Store Bath Supplies

Bathroom accessories – those humble utilitarian aids so necessary to daily life – are frequently a challenge to store. Some items definitely belong in a drawer, others deserve a pedestal. Properly displayed, such everyday necessities as soap and bath gel can be appreciated for their simple beauty. Be creative in your choice of containers. Borrow bowls from the kitchen, buckets from the garden, teacups from the china cabinet, a silver platter from the dining room. Vintage enamelware is especially practical for the bath. It comes in a variety of shapes and sizes, and it's durable, colorful, and water resistant.

A slender glass vase, *above*, fitted with a slotted cover marries toothbrushes and toothpaste.
A sampling of bath soaps, *right*, find a home together in a fluted enamelware jelly mold. A tidy profusion of soaps in open containers can subtly scent the small space of a bathroom.

A glass compote, *left*, makes soap a sublime bathroom centerpiece. To create an arrangement of your own, play with sizes and shapes: nestle tiny guest soaps against manor-size bars. White on white accentuates the purity of a sparkling clean bath, but soaps can be grouped to dramatic effect in any number of ways. Choose your favorites, then use your imagination. **Bath supplies look beautiful**, *below*, decanted into matching bottles. Clear containers make it easy to identify contents; add homemade labels for a personal touch.

Hooks mounted on chalkboards, *above*, let you personalize storage spots for each household member and leave messages where they are sure to be read. To cut down on confusion, consider assigning each bathroom or each person a towel color. Monograms are another classic and efficient way to identify towels; have names or initials embroidered on each set. **A gently weathered wood screen**, *right*, turns into a freestanding towel rack when placed by a sunny window to speed drying. Freshly laundered towels can be draped over a towel rack, hung from hooks, or rolled into colorful rosettes and stacked on a shelf. Hand towels, face towels, and washcloths can be rolled or folded into squares and arranged in baskets or stacked on chairs.

How to Store Towels

Towels are meant to be seen and used. They are the natural grace notes in a bathroom, necessities that add color and texture. As luxuries with an everyday role to play, they are a daily comfort to you and a sign of hospitality to guests. Care for them as well as they care for you. Rotate your stock so that towels are evenly used throughout the year. Give damp towels plenty of time to dry before you toss them in the hamper, and give clean ones plenty of room to breathe in linen closets or bathroom cabinets. The most efficient way to prepare towels for storage is to fold them in thirds lengthwise and then fold them in thirds again.

A handsome tray, *left*, or a basket carryall can serve up a fresh set of towels, soaps, loofahs, and bath gel when guests are expected. It makes a generous show of welcome and is an easy way to carry essentials from guest room to bath and back again. **A ladder-back chair**, *above*, lets you store towels in a corner and offers a "seat" for bath supplies. Damp towels need special treatment. Hang them straight, preferably from a bar or a rod rather than a hook, to expose more surface to circulating air. Allow at least two inches between towel and wall to prevent mildew, and avoid hanging wet towels together for the same reason. The possibilities for displaying and storing towels are as limitless as your imagination.

laundry rooms

Once upon a time, laundry day came once a week and the laundry took all day. Although modern washing has become more convenient, many laundry rooms remain a little behind the times. If your laundry room feels more like a catchall jumble than a streamlined workstation, a new routine is in order. Despite the piles of wash and stacks of ironing, a makeover is easier than you may think. Even if you don't have a full-fledged laundry room, you can transform a basement corner or a converted closet into a wash space with style.

Detergent and fabric softener should be kept above or near the washing machine in containers small enough to handily pour liquid or to scoop powder; keep dryer sheets within comfortable reach of the dryer. If you have a little extra space, consider adding a "stain-removal center" and a tool kit for quick hemming and mending jobs. If space is tight, keep stain-removal products next to the washer in a small, wall-mounted cabinet.

Next, make sure your ironing board or folding table is at a height that's comfortable for you to work. Creating an all-in-one ironing center can be

The laundry room is often the most neglected space in the entire house. Give yours a fresh look with storage that's as stylish and inviting as it is hardworking.

Address practical needs first. Aim for a layout that's bright and functional. First and foremost, this means sufficient lighting and easy-to-clean painted finishes in white or a fresh, light color. (You can use deck paint to seal floors and make other surfaces water resistant.) If you're starting from scratch, deep sinks, roomy cabinets, and a long countertop for folding and sorting clothes are great features to build in. If you're working with what you've got, then having (or adding) enough easy-access storage to keep laundry supplies organized is chief among the essentials. Begin with sturdy, open shelving, and arrange products according to the way you use them.

as simple as setting up an adjustable ironing board – freestanding or wall mounted – fitted with a metal rack for the iron, and a hanging rod nearby for freshly pressed clothing.

Keep an assortment of sturdy plastic bins and containers close at hand for presoaking extra-dirty items and for gathering articles to be sent to the dry cleaner. Add a few versatile extras such as wall hooks for hanging stray socks or just-pressed shirts, or a collapsible wooden rack for drying sweaters or rain-soaked outerwear. Store supplies in vessels and containers that are pleasing to the eye. Give everyday chores a stylish setting and make your laundry a pleasurable place to be.

A Well-Appointed Laundry Room

Even behind-the-scenes places like a laundry room can be attractive and comfortable. Paint the walls with a cool sweep of color and choose storage that's as decorative as it is useful. Add witty accents that turn a hardworking space into a stylish one. It's all in the details.

When decorating your home, the laundry room is easy to overlook. But, in this most practical of spaces, a quick makeover can add a measure of delight to wash day. A playful approach to storage makes all the difference here, where all work and no fun is generally the rule.

Identify all of your usual laundry tasks – from sorting and spot cleaning to washing and drying delicates – and choose storage accordingly. Start with matching containers placed to keep necessities at the ready. Glass jars look clean, offer a clear view of their contents, and help keep small items out of jumbled drawers (consider candy jars, vases, or kitchen canisters). A strategically placed basket can hide rags and sponges from view. A wall-mounted clip rack for drying delicates keeps the countertop clear.

Anticipate laundry emergencies and outfit a special kit for stain removal and clothing repair. If possible, arrange this "first aid" station near a sink, and stock it with as many cleaning provisions as possible: a squeeze bottle of diluted dishwashing liquid for juice and jam spills, a scoop and a bowl of sea salt for wine stains, an atomizer filled with hairspray or rubbing alcohol for removing ink spots.

Metal mailboxes, *left*, rescue items found in pockets and keep them out of the washing machine. A wall-mounted clipboard, *right*, hangs small items to dry near the sink. Make laundry storage look pretty by pouring detergent and fabric softener into clear plastic or glass containers.

To make each laundry task easier, place open-access storage on walls as well as shelves. Clips or pegs over the washing machine can catch stray socks, keys, and clothing care labels. Decant detergents and softeners into sturdy, clear containers that are small enough to handle and pour with ease. Apothecary bottles are perfect for the job and add colorful accents. Enamel flower pails stand up to the humid atmosphere and are attractive organizers for spray starch, distilled water, and dryer sheets.

A portable sewing kit, *above*, is ready for emergency mending. Extra buttons, needles, and thread are kept tidy in clear spice jars on a brightly colored tray. **Floor-to-ceiling storage**, *right*, makes room for enamel pails, baskets of rolled towels, and bottles of laundry detergent, all placed within comfortable reach. An antique medicine cabinet displays supplies for stain removal: soda water, vinegar, sea salt, towelettes, and a mini-washboard.

Design Details

Color Palette

A color combination that immediately signifies fresh, clean laundry and softly scented linens, pale shades of blue, green, and lavender come together to make this laundry room an inviting oasis. With walls painted in a shade of pale blue-green, the white appliances and storage units stand out in clean contrast. Splashes of brighter blue-green, sky blue, and mint green found in enameled accessories mimic the classic colors of decanted detergent, softener, and stain removers.

Where space allows, provide an area for sorting clothes before washing and one for folding clean items. If there is a long section of wall, you may wish to tuck large bins or rolling carts (one each for whites, colors, and delicates) under a waist-high table. Make sure that laundry bins are lightweight enough to transport easily. If space is tight, install a fold-down shelf or ironing board. Or, use a rack that fits behind a door or on a wall to keep the ironing board out of the way when not in use. Don't just think of storage in terms of floor and cabinet space. Take advantage of wall space by gluing on clothespins to hang drying or just-ironed clothing.

Storage and Care

Irons are best stored in a heat-resistant cubby or on a shelf wide enough to keep a hot iron secure from falling. Never store near fabric or on a painted surface. Set atop a stone tile, trivet, or other non-flammable surface. For long-term storage, empty of water and let air-dry before wrapping the cord around the iron.

Detergent looks best when it's transferred into decorative containers. Decant liquid detergent into glass or plastic bottles for easy pouring. Pour the powder variety into a lidded jar or cannister and add a scoop. Or, hide the entire box or bottle of detergent within a decorative tin or box.

Scrub brushes should be kept in plastic, ceramic, or stone dishes with holes for water to drain — repurposed flower pots are a good choice. Completely dry brushes may be stored in wooden drawer inserts.

Sorting bins, *left*, with removable canvas bags slip under a table in this busy laundry workstation. The tabletop is perfect for small ironing jobs and for folding clothes. A freshly pressed blouse hangs on a clothespin cleverly affixed to the wall. **Wide-mouth jars**, *above*, make ideal storage containers for clothespins or dryer sheets.

Hideaway Laundry

An upstairs washer and dryer is a luxury anyone can appreciate. And contrary to what you might expect, it doesn't require a spare room – only an extra closet and a little strategic planning.

Nothing compares to the convenience of a laundry tucked into a closet just steps away from bed and bath. While a washer and dryer take up minimal square footage, most closets will require a few expert adjustments to install the laundry room necessities of proper plumbing and ventilation.

To make your laundry "room" as efficient as possible, retain the closet rod for freshly pressed garments and add shelves for cleaning supplies. A stacked washer and dryer works best for smaller closets or to create extra room for laundry sorting bins.

Detergents and solutions, *left*, have been decanted into clear containers so they're more attractive and easy to use. **Clothing care tags and repair supplies**, *above*, slip into the plastic pockets of a notebook. **Sliding doors**, *right*, keep this laundry closet hidden away when not in use.

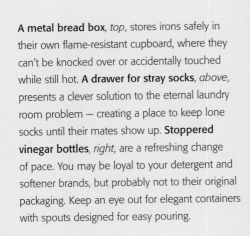

A metal bread box, *top*, stores irons safely in their own flame-resistant cupboard, where they can't be knocked over or accidentally touched while still hot. A drawer for stray socks, *above*, presents a clever solution to the eternal laundry room problem — creating a place to keep lone socks until their mates show up. Stoppered vinegar bottles, *right*, are a refreshing change of pace. You may be loyal to your detergent and softener brands, but probably not to their original packaging. Keep an eye out for elegant containers with spouts designed for easy pouring.

How to Organize a Laundry Room

A well-stocked laundry room is a little like a well-stocked cupboard. Both have a comforting air of "all's right with the world." Keep things in order with a few imaginative storage solutions, and treat your laundry room to a touch of style at the same time. Place everything you regularly use near the washing machine, and arrange products in the order that you use them: stain treatments, washing powders or liquids, softeners, and dryer sheets. Install a rod or hook on which to hang clothes as you iron, and a folding table or fold-down shelf near the dryer.

A "first-aid kit" for stain removal, *left*, puts everything you need for tough laundry jobs in one place. Keep it stocked with modern stain sticks and such old-fashioned remedies as seltzer, baking soda, bar soap, blotting cloths, and scrub brushes. For good measure, include a list of stain-removal tips inside as well. **Borrow from the kitchen**, *above*, to find containers perfect for storing laundry detergents and supplies. The size, weight, and wide mouths of kitchen canisters are as well suited to powdered detergent and clothespins as they are to flour and sugar. Or, use enameled tin jars with tight-fitting lids, which can be found at many kitchen supply stores.

utility rooms

Not everyone has the space for a utility room, but every home should have a utility area – a closet, a wall of shelves, or even just a countertop and a few drawers where tools, glue, lightbulbs, and batteries can be stored and retrieved with ease. Whether your utility "room" is a whole garage, a shared space, or a few containers tucked in a closet, making the most of it depends on specialized storage.

Think of your utility room as the family warehouse. It's the place where you keep things you may not use every day but don't want to search

of the available space. One option is to subdivide your collection into heavy and light, inside and outside, dry and wet categories. If you've amassed a daunting assortment of unmarked tins and left-over paints, label and keep the paint colors you still have in your house and safely dispose of the rest to make room for fresh supplies.

Before you sink a nail or hang a shelf, take a look at the larger setting and decide whether it could use a bit of improving first. A simple patch-and-paint job and a modest investment in new overhead lighting can transform a dreary garage

A house without a dedicated utility space is like a toolbox without compartments. Sure, you know where the nuts and bolts are; it's just a lot harder to find them.

for when you really need them: duct tape, gift wrapping paper for the holidays, hammers, nails, tape measures, extra bags for the vacuum cleaner, lighter fluid for the barbecue. The items in this list have one thing in common: they are usually found jammed into the most likely but least convenient space – boxed up in the basement or garage, or in the attic reached by a drop-down ladder. If so, it may be time for a change.

Take a weekend, turn on some favorite music, pull every household handyman tool, gadget, and mystery solvent from its hiding place, sort it by type, and make a rough inventory. If household tools predominate, assign them the largest section

or basement room into a cheerful work center in no time. Then hang shelves and pegboard and decide what goes where. Use modular storage pieces to create perfectly sized compartments for items large and small. If you have the room, a worktable is a luxury in a utility room – a place to wrap presents, fix things, cut flowers, or work on projects. For narrow or odd-shaped spaces, you can craft a custom table from a couple of sawhorses topped with wooden planks sanded smooth. Midsized items can be stashed in plastic milk crates or galvanized bins and stored under the worktable; bulky gadgets can be lined up along a free wall, according to size or function.

Everything in Working Order

A no-nonsense utility room is a thing of beauty. It's a pleasure to work surrounded by neat rows of tools and supplies. A well-stocked and organized workroom helps you stay on top of everyday chores, frees up space elsewhere in the house, and makes each day go more smoothly.

If you have the space in a garage, basement, spare room, or attic, you have the opportunity to create a dedicated utility room. All it requires is a little pegboard and paint, and some skill at sorting and separating. Start by listing items that can be stored apart from where they might be used: large containers of cleaning liquid, for example, or such seldom-used tools as a floor buffer. Make a separate inventory of jobs you'd like to be able to do in the workroom. (Combining a wood shop with an indoor potting shed in a single space may be a good idea; combining it with a sewing center may not be.) Plan for the type of flooring and lighting that are the most practical for your needs, and decide whether the room requires soundproofing.

Now imagine yourself at work in the room, reaching for a tool you need. Pegboard is the ideal material for displaying and organizing tools: no more rummaging in a cluttered toolbox for the Phillips-head screwdriver or the needlenose pliers. If your workroom is shared, you can make it more convenient for users to return tools to their correct places by outlining the shape of each tool on the pegboard.

Painted red for energy, *left and right*, pegboard brightens the atmosphere of this workroom. At left, a wall cubby sorts wrapping paper, and curtain rods dispense drawing and kraft paper. **A spice rack and glass spice jars**, *right*, make perfect storage for such easy-to-lose, easy-to-confuse items as nuts and bolts, screws and hooks. Wrenches, pliers, and screwdrivers in graduated sizes stay handy and organized when hung against a brightly colored board.

One side of this multipurpose utility room is devoted to household tools and craft projects, the other to gardening equipment and supplies. Along the wall, a deep built-in desk is framed by a pair of cupboards and a row of upper cabinets that offer closed storage and give the room a finished appearance. Twin wood worktables placed in the center of the room are a comfortable height for standing while working.

Cheerful colors and open workstations create an inviting utility room for family projects.

Pull-out work surfaces on the tables allow more than one person to work at each station, while drawers underneath keep materials close at hand. Lower shelves provide even more storage space. Wall-hung clipboards hold seasonal to-do lists for house, garden, and garage. Easily misplaced paint chips and fabric swatches are filed in hanging wall racks for ready reference.

Practical task lighting is just one of the simple details that makes this utility room run smoothly. Drawers in the work bench store files and tools. To prevent things from getting lost in deep drawers, fit them with baskets that you can remove and use as supply bins for each project.

Design Details

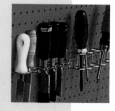

Color Palette

While orange is commonly thought of as the color of work and safety, an energetic shade of tomato red can create a similar effect with some added style for an all-purpose utility room. Here, panels of pegboard are painted a bright shade of red-orange to call attention to a wall of tools. The golden tones of the wooden tables and interior of the built-in cabinet suggest the warmth and hand-crafted quality of a woodshop. The cool glint of stainless steel in the pendant lights and tools calls to mind an industrial workroom.

Storage and Care

Metal tools are best kept in drawers or compartments that keep them clean and dry. Store all sharp tools with blades facing the same direction. A tool chest is an ideal storage area, but for frequently used tools, pegboard allows them to be placed over a worktable within convenient reach.

Paintbrushes should be stored flat, side by side in shallow boxes or drawers, in order to keep bristles flat and without stress. Always store brushes after they have been properly cleaned and dried.

Garden tools should be stored clean. Wall hooks work well for organization and quick and easy access. Drawers, bins, or baskets are good, but keep these in dry areas to protect metal from rusting and wood handles from rotting. Store pruning shears and other bladed tools in a protective leather sheath.

An indoor potting shed may seem like an oxymoron, but this streamlined setup proves otherwise. In a built-in cupboard, spacious overhead shelves store clay pots and car-washing supplies. A deep sink for transplanting and watering keeps messy garden chores out of the kitchen. Beneath the sink, grass seed and fertilizer are stored in galvanized steel trash cans that can be carried outdoors as needed. The freestanding table offers additional storage and room for more than one person to work at a time.

A large hideaway cabinet, *left,* allows bulky gardening items such as clay pots, grass seed, and fertilizer to be stored away for the season. **Frequently used small tools and supplies**, *above,* can be left out on a countertop when organized in easily moveable trays.

Essentials for an Organized Attic

The image of the attic as a household museum is hard to shake. But if you've been wanting a little extra space for all sorts of projects, consider closing the exhibit and setting up shop. Start with ingenious storage ideas that echo the attic's eclectic sense of history.

Not so long ago, obsolete items were relegated to the attic and promptly forgotten, providing children with a place to spend a memorable rainy day. If you're eager to add more living space to the house, employ the neglected space upstairs. Give your attic a makeover that will put it back in circulation and make it a destination for homework, craft projects, or simply getting things organized.

If your attic has proper floors, heating, electrical outlets, and good ventilation, you could set up a simple, comfortable workspace for creative projects. Even an unfinished attic room can be put to work as a storage area with the addition of a fresh coat of paint, plenty of easy-to-read labels, and easily assembled wire shelving (when planning an attic overhaul, the last thing you want to worry about is carting large pieces of furniture upstairs).

The first step is to sort through the attic's current contents, editing out items that have neither practical nor sentimental value. Catalog all the things you want to save and sort them by size and function. Set aside promising recyclables – intact pieces of shelving, carts on wheels, or empty file cabinets. Keep an eye out for useful containers as you go.

Wine crates and a vintage suitcase, *left*, mix easily with more modern containers. European-style house numbers indexed to a storage log help you keep track of contents. **A pair of rolling tennis-ball caddies**, *right*, serve as mobile bins for mail supplies and packing material in this attic's project area.

A large part of an attic's charm is the history and well-worn beauty of the things it houses. Mixing old with new is an attractive (and practical) approach to attic storage. Organize your favorite keepsakes on wire-gauge shelving. The grid of the shelves lets air circulate around boxes, a must for preserving items in long-term storage. If the ventilation in your attic is poor, consider adding a ceiling or vent fan.

Using recycled treasures and found containers makes attic storage both personal and practical.

If you have adequate air circulation, not everything needs to be in modern storage boxes. As long as they are well constructed, many types of containers will do. Store large and less frequently used items on upper shelves, more frequently used items down lower, and place fragile items in a single row to protect contents from being crushed. Take the time to make easy-to-read labels, or use see-through containers to identify contents at a quick glance.

A weathered flower-market cart, *left*, finds new life as an all-in-one gift wrapping station. Antique leather cases hold tape, string, ribbons, and scissors. **A ready-to-toss table base**, *right*, becomes a useful work surface when topped with unfinished wooden planks.

A great part of an attic's appeal is its air of possibility. The well-stocked attic filled with still-serviceable pieces can be a repurposing gold mine. A desk, pieced together from the frame of an old dining table and a few weathered planks, might make a comfortable place to label and catalogue items, wrap packages, or enjoy craft projects on a rainy afternoon. Imaginative recycling transforms a paper towel holder into a tape rack or a wire bicycle basket into a supply cage. An old galvanized tin tray fitted with a few colorful spare knobs becomes an amusing spot for storing keys and other odds and ends.

For quick retrieval of boxed items, *left*, take Polaroids of each container's contents and use them to create a master log in a scrapbook. **An overturned bicycle basket**, *above*, makes an efficient string dispenser and scissors holder.

Design Details

Color Palette

A quick coat of white paint can do wonders to make any room fresh and ready for action. In this attic, a neutral palette of white and shades of beige and gray turns an unused space into an inviting blank "canvas" for home projects. When sunlight is at a premium, white or other bright colors reflect light and make the most of scant exposure. The industrial glint of stainless steel — in the wire shelving and vintage office chair — and the patina of worn wood reveal the hardworking nature of this multipurpose utility room.

Storage and Care

Papers and documents are best kept in fire-resistant cabinets or a safe-deposit box if they are irreplaceable. They can also be stored in polypropylene sheet protectors within a binder with acid-free page backs, or in archival storage boxes that will protect the paper from breaking down. Maps should be stored flat in shallow drawers.

Mementos should be kept in sturdy wooden boxes or in archival boxes lined with acid-free paper. Wrap delicate items in tissue or cushion them with packing material. Preserve mementos by keeping them out of sunlight, in a cool, dry space.

Delicate holiday ornaments should ideally be stored in shallow plastic boxes or sturdy cardboard boxes, each one wrapped in tissue or nested in packing material. Remove hooks before storing glass ornaments to prevent scratches.

How to Organize a Mudroom

Putting on a few pieces of brightly colored clothing can brighten things up on a rainy day. If you are provisioning a mudroom, you can benefit from this bit of practical wisdom; a few well-chosen splashes of color can elevate the lowly but essential mudroom and transform it into a friendly buffer zone between indoors and out. The formula for furnishings is simple: supply ample seating for struggling boot-tuggers, and include enough hooks and baskets to sort mittens, scarves, umbrellas, hats, and foul-weather gear. Keep furnishings and accessories bright, and add a few amusing accents to make friends and family smile.

Colorful canvas bags, *above,* can relieve tabletops and benches of accumulated clutter and make even a "last-minute guest" cleanup a snap. Use them to store mittens and scarves, leashes, mail and magazines, insect repellent and sunscreen, or school books. Anything that can be hung above the fray in a mudroom is a plus, because it frees up space at ground level for dressing and undressing. **Roomy baskets,** *right,* make another wise storage solution. They're easy to find when another pair of mittens is needed (use clothespins to clip pairs together and discourage rummaging), easy to fill quickly when it's time to tidy up, and just as easily moved out of sight when you want a ready-for-company look.

Mismatched metals, *left*, in a vintage milk jug and planter line up to serve as good-humored umbrella stands, transforming a foul-weather necessity into colorful art. The most direct path to establishing order in a mudroom is an assigned place for everything, with particular attention paid to wet items. Be sure to have hooks or pegs where damp articles can air-dry, and choose durable materials that can stand up to rain-soaked gear. **A perfectly measured coat cubby**, *above*, incorporates a small bench to sit on while removing boots (well protected by several coats of varnish), hooks for hanging dripping raincoats and jackets, and overhead cupboards for hideaway storage.

Room Resources

At Pottery Barn, we believe that casual style is something you can weave through every space in your home, from front rooms to private havens. For this book, we scoured hundreds of locations to find perfect settings to create rooms just for you. We experimented with colors, furnishings, rugs, drapes, and accessories to find the best combinations for each space. The results? This collection of style ideas, which we hope will inspire and delight you.

Each location chosen for this book was unique and interesting. Here is a little bit more about each of the homes we visited, the style ideas we created, and the individual elements that make each design tick.

A note about color: wherever it was possible in this list of resources, we've offered the actual paint manufacturer and paint color that was used in the room shown. We also list the closest Benjamin Moore paint color match (in parentheses). Because photography and color printing processes can dramatically change the way colors appear, it is very important to test swatches of any paint color you are considering in your own home, where you can see how the light affects them at different times of the day.

Balancing Storage and Display

Designed in 1931 by California architect William Wurster, this stuccoed house overlooks a garden attributed to landscape designer Thomas Church.

Space The 14' x 19' living room has exposed clear heart redwood beams and ceilings. The room has a built-in mural by painter Henrietta Shore, a student of Georgia O'Keefe. Floors are ebonized oak throughout the house.

Color Walls are papered in grass paper. Shelves (Benjamin Moore Old Prairie 1521 semigloss).

Furnishings Manhattan leather chair, Westport sofa in twill, Metropolitan tables and console, Benares rug, Savannah baskets, Voluminous vases, velvet pillows in wheat, and linen tufted pillows in sage, all from Pottery Barn.

Lighting Rio lamp with square silk shade from Pottery Barn.

Display Zambian wedding basket. Gallery frames from Pottery Barn mixed with vintage frames.

pages 16–21

Elements of an Entryway

Set on a hillside with picturesque mountain views, this spacious home is part of an estate that includes a pool and vineyard. The entryway opens onto a gracious wraparound porch.

Space The high-ceilinged entryway leads to a spacious kitchen and great room. Walls and ceilings are paneled and wash-painted white in the style of a country farmhouse.

Color Walls and ceiling Fuller O'Brien White Wing flat (Benjamin Moore White Heron OC-57).

Furnishings Cabot console and bench, Colorbound seagrass runner, Samantha baskets, and tufted velvet pillows, all from Pottery Barn. Vintage hotel laundry hamper, silver toast holder, galvanized metal tray, wooden shaving soap bowls, ceramic paint-mixing cups, and wooden garden trug.

Lighting Wood paneled ceiling has recessed lighting, including several flip-down picture lights.

Display Collection of straw hats.

pages 26–29

Living with Books

California architect John Marsh Davis designed this house and set it in a shady grove of pines, madrone, and laurel. Recovered redwood beams and wood trim are throughout the house.

Space The library is at the end of the house, away from the noise and traffic of the open-plan kitchen-dining-living space. Custom-designed redwood bookcases line the room. The fireplace in the library has a steel surround. Floors are tiled in red slate.

Color Walls (Benjamin Moore Rainforest Dew 2146-50 satin).

Furnishings Charleston chairs, Manhattan leather ottoman, Schoolhouse chair, Bedford system modular desk, Henley rug, Melange Gabbeh rug, Metropolitan console table, Folsom leather totes, three-button velvet pillows, chenille throw, and shadow box frames, all from Pottery Barn. Chalk-board garden markers from Smith & Hawken.

Lighting Apothecary lamps from Pottery Barn.

Display Turn-of-the-century leather-bound and clothbound first-edition books.

pages 38–45

Cool, Calm, and Collected

On a quiet suburban street, this two-story gabled and shingled cottage hides behind tall hedges. The front porch overlooks an English garden; flowering borders and climbing roses edge the lawn.

Space The family room shares space with a modern kitchen and rustically decorated dining area. French doors open to the outside, where an electric train set, complete with bridges and village, rings a tree in the backyard.

Color Walls (Benjamin Moore Leisure Green 2035-60 flat).

Furnishings PB Basic square-arm sofa, velvet tuffets, Cabot coffee table, Picadilly rug, swivel desk chair, and Metropolitan corkboard, all from Pottery Barn. Wall-mounted magazine racks. Stackable wooden storage boxes. Canvas toy-storage bin. Aluminum paint-mixing cans.

Lighting Recessed ceiling lights.

pages 60–65

Making Room for Media

Amid palm and banana trees, this Mediterranean-style villa overlooks a courtyard and is flanked by a small, serene garden. A guest house and studio cottage share the property with the main building.

Space This family media room measures a cozy 11' x 11' but is surprisingly airy and light thanks to 8' French doors that open onto a garden on one side and a backyard patio on the other. Floors and wood trim are mahogany throughout. (Contact www.smartwood.org to learn more about responsibly harvested rare woods like these.)

Color Walls (Benjamin Moore Simply White 2143-70 flat).

Furnishings Folsom leather tote, and Henley rug, all from Pottery Barn. Clear magazine, CD, and DVD storage boxes from Hold Everything. Vintage turned wood collection and metal film reel canisters.

Lighting Recessed ceiling lights.

Display Fujitsu plasma screen TV mounted on wall.

pages 66–69

Organizing an Eat-in Kitchen

A Spanish-style villa with a modern twist, this house has a stucco facade with a Gothic window, and a traditional courtyard with a pool, guest house, and project studio.

Space Long and narrow, the kitchen measures 13' x 32' and has a small balcony that overlooks the rear courtyard and pool. A built-in office nook is tucked into one of the floor-to-ceiling cupboards; a pantry is hidden in another.

Color Walls (Benjamin Moore Grant Beige HC-83 flat).

Furnishings Hotel dinner napkins, Sausalito dinnerware, Audrey silverware, Springwood salad bowls and wood tray, all from Pottery Barn. Circa 1900 French bottle-drying rack. Vintage French pickling jar holds wooden utensils.

Lighting Recessed halogen cove and task lighting.

Display Vintage French clock-tower clock.

pages 80–85

Concealed and Revealed

Built in 1931, this long, rambling house perches on a steep hillside, on land that was once part of the 15,000-acre Vicente Spanish land grant. The house overlooks a landmark 1915 resort and spa.

Space Twin banks of corner windows take in hillside views, blurring the distinction between inside and out. The bedroom opens onto a tiny art studio and balcony. Floors are ebonized oak.

Color Walls (Benjamin Moore Guilford Green1509 flat).

Furnishings Sumatra bed, Basic Hemstitch duvet cover, shams, and bedding, Ally silk quilt and shams, Ticking Stripe bedding (under bed), Greenwich armchairs in brushed twill, velvet tufted pillow, Garrison secretary, Sylvan stools, Ginger square tables, hammered metal trays, leather-wrapped candles, Frameless oval mirror, and Savannah baskets, all from Pottery Barn. Custom-built cherry, mahogany, and oak trays with casters, for under-bed storage, designed by Lee Battorff.

Lighting Pharmacy lamps from Pottery Barn.

Display Black-and-white photography by Heather Reid.

pages 94–99

Storage for a Restful Space

Formerly a 1950s ranch house, this building was completely redesigned and rebuilt in 1999. In the modern living room, floor-to-ceiling retractable glass doors offer views of Mount Tamalpais and the San Francisco Bay.

Space The house is 6,500 square feet. Architecture by Fu-Tung Cheng, Cheng Design, San Francisco. Interior design by Paul Levinson Design, San Francisco (restyled by Pottery Barn for photos).

Color Walls (Benjamin Moore Minced Onion 2145-60 and Benjamin Moore Rich Cream 2153-60 semigloss).

Furnishings Cameron bookcases (bed platform) from PB Kids. Slipcovered headboard, Grand bedding shams and duvet cover in fawn, beaded silk pillows, Savannah baskets, Maxime cube in twill, abaca runner, Westport chaise, Westport armless chair, chenille throw, and tufted linen pillows, all from Pottery Barn. Bookcase from Hold Everything.

Lighting Drum shades from PB Teen. Eureka recessed LV directional lights.

pages 100–103

Planning a Walk-in Closet

This villa-style home is sited high on a suburban hillside. It has a stucco exterior, terraced front entrance, and a secluded rear courtyard, which is the site of a private guest house and a swimming pool.

Space The walk-in closet opens from the master bedroom and has a full-size window seat with views of the tropical plants and pool in the rear courtyard. Its sturdy, seagrass wall-to-wall carpeting was installed for durability and to feel good under bare feet.

Color Walls (Benjamin Moore Beacon Hill Damask HC-2 semigloss).

Furnishings Rattan laundry basket, solid twill pillow, and Sierra stripe pillow, all from Pottery Barn. Cotton canvas storage boxes, cotton canvas hanging storage bags, large suit hanger with rod, shirt hanger, shirt hanger with clips, women's shirt hanger, padded hanger, and pants clamps, all from Hold Everything. Vintage glove forms and wood frame mirrors.

Lighting Built-in chrome base table lamps, recessed ceiling lights.

pages 110–15

A Master Plan for a Master Bath

Designed by an architect for his own family, the style of this house and its courtyard was inspired by an old Florida estate. There are no hallways on the first floor, so each room flows into the next.

Space The house is narrow, to offer every room a view of either the front garden courtyard or the backyard. This bathroom's window trim, shelves, and custom-built cabinets are mahogany, to match the mahogany floors that are throughout the house. Windows are based on a 1920s design; screens lower from a pocket in the upper portion of the window. Countertops and tub surround are limestone.

Color Walls (Benjamin Moore Simply White 2143-70 semigloss).

Furnishings Essential towels, Classic plush bath mat, Monaco glass bowl and glass cylinder vases, all from Pottery Barn.

Lighting Skylights and sconce lights.

pages 128–33

Storage Solutions for a Family Bath

This newly built shingled cottage was designed for a busy family with children. The first floor includes a room dedicated to arts and crafts projects and a spacious kitchen-dining-den area.

Space The floor is hexagonal tile, an option that offers plenty of traction thanks to the many areas of grout between each small tile. The gloss paint finish on paneled and wainscot surfaces repels moisture and makes them easy to clean.

Color Walls (Benjamin Moore Windmill Wings 2067-60 semigloss).

Furnishings Essential towels, Classic plush bath mat, chrome wall hooks, component curtain rod, and etched glass ball finials, all from Pottery Barn. Peyton step stool from PB Kids. Console lavatory, 72" reproduction claw-foot tub with reproduction Victorian fittings. Toy schoolroom chalkboards.

Lighting Sconce lights and recessed ceiling lights.

pages 134–37

Storage on Display

Craftsman and bungalow details are combined in the classic lines of this new house. Built on a large lot that formerly held four buildings, the house has front and back porches, and passageways connecting kids' rooms and playrooms.

Space The limestone counters and cherry-stained alder cabinets are custom-built. The homeowner chose alder over cherry wood due to its superior hardness and resistance to yellowing. The bathtub platform is cherry-stained oak.

Color Walls (Benjamin Moore Putnam Ivory HC-39).

Furnishings Monogrammed robes, Essential towels, heathered bath towels, braided chenille rug, Roman shades, towel ring, glass cylinder vase, pillar candles, Frameless oval mirror all from Pottery Barn. Vintage tub and Antique tub fittings by Kohler. Sinks by Toto, sink fittings by Grohe. Custom cabinetry by Finish Line Cabinets, Santa Ana, CA.

Lighting Skylights and recessed ceiling lights.

Display Vintage fashion sketches and circa 1930s metal signs.

pages 138–45

A Well-Appointed Laundry Room

This angular, modern home was built to replace a three-story Tudor that burned in summer fires. Walls of windows offer sweeping, 360-degree views of the hillside and the Pacific Ocean from many rooms.

Space Located adjacent to a home office and catwalk that leads to the master bedroom, the laundry room is 11' x 6'. Open shelves are 1.5' tall by 2.8' wide, to easily accommodate large containers of cleaning supplies.

Color Walls (Benjamin Moore Blue Bonnet 2050-70).

Furnishings Samantha baskets, Essential towels, and wall-mounted Grand phone, all from Pottery Barn. Laundry sorter from Hold Everything. Vintage enamel buckets and tray. Vintage first-aid cabinet.

Display Circa 1920s laundry sign and circa 1940s magazine ad.

pages 154–59

Everything in Working Order

In the oasis of a tiled courtyard planted with bougainvillea and palm and banana trees, the three buildings of this villa overlook a fountain. The roof of the main house is terra-cotta tile.

Space The utility center is one of three buildings on this property. It is 500 square feet, as is the guest house with which it shares the front courtyard. The main house is 2,700 square feet.

Color Walls (Benjamin Moore Simply White 2143-70 flat). Pegboards (Benjamin Moore Tropical Orange 2170-20).

Furnishings Ashland Collection project tables, Haley bench, Swivel desk chair, component curtain rod, and Samantha baskets, all from Pottery Barn. Steel locker bins from PB Teen.

Lighting Ceiling fixtures.

pages 168–73

Essentials for an Organized Attic

On a busy urban street, this three-story Victorian townhouse has a small, top-story deck that overlooks rooftops and the city below. Twelve-foot ceilings give the interior an Old World atmosphere.

Space The refurbished attic has a painted brick chimney that acts as an informal divider in the space. The room is 16 square feet, with storage dedicated to one side of the chimney and a guest bedroom set up on the other.

Color Walls and ceilings (Benjamin Moore Mountain Peak White 2148-70 semigloss).

Furnishings Stainless steel baker's shelving. Collection of vintage suitcases used for storage. Wooden wine crates. Acid-neutral archival boxes with reinforced corners. Vintage chocolate drop packaging. Antique French flower seller's cart and metal table base. Circa 1950s metal swivel chair. Wire sports equipment caddies and bicycle basket.

Lighting Suspended uplight ceiling fixtures.

pages 174–79

Glossary

Acid-free paper and tissue Paper that has had the acid removed from the pulp is best for storing documents, photographs, letters, and artwork. Placing layers of acid-free paper or tissue between items helps slow the deterioration of stored papers because it forms a barrier between the documents and their container or the air.

Alder A wood with a straight, fine grain, American alder is widely used to make furniture. It was once the lumber most commonly used in the U.S., mostly for structural purposes. Alder ages to a golden brown or reddish tan.

Apothecary jars These glass containers take their name from pharmacies – once called apothecaries – and are appealing for their old-fashioned shapes and rich colors. Amber, cobalt, and green glass were commonly used because they blocked sunlight that could damage the potency of medicinal contents.

Architectural salvage Antique or recovered parts of a building, including decorative moulding, columns, millwork, corbels, cornices, and window sashes. Architectural salvage has become a collectible accessory that adds a fanciful and unique touch to a room's decor.

Archive A collection of valuable papers and objects is ideally preserved in an archive, or repository, protected from light, heat, dust, and moisture. Archival boxes and paper are specially designed to protect valuable documents.

Armoire A large cupboard or wardrobe with doors, the armoire has been used since medieval times to contain clothing. The French term "armoire" originally referred to a piece of furniture in which armor was stored. Modern-day armoires are well suited to hold clothing, a TV, dinnerware, or even a compact office.

Atomizer A device that sprays liquid as a fine mist, an atomizer is often attached to bottles of perfume and cologne. Atomizers can be used in a variety of ways in the kitchen, laundry, and bath.

Beaker A tall, open-mouthed vessel used in a chemist's laboratory for storing and pouring liquids. Beakers are made of tempered clear glass and usually have etched lines intended for measuring.

Built-in storage Fabricated specifically for a particular space, built-in storage, whether cabinetry or shelving, is designed to be part of a room's architecture. By fitting precisely into a wall, built-in storage takes up less floor space than freestanding storage and helps to cut down on visual clutter.

Butler's pantry A small, separate room between the kitchen and dining room in which plates, glassware, and other dining accessories were traditionally stored.

Cachepot A decorative container intended to hide a flowerpot, a cachepot may be ceramic, metal, or wood.

Canvas This heavy-duty fabric is most commonly used for manufacturing sporting goods, awnings, and outdoor furnishing. When used for drapes, slipcovers, or pillows, it brings a casual and relaxed feel to a room. Canvas can be made from linen, hemp, or cotton and is available bleached, unbleached, or in a variety of dyed hues.

Cedar The type of wood used to make the linings of chests and drawers, hangers, and blocks or balls to tuck into drawers. Because of its fragrance and moth-repellent qualities, cedar (mostly North American red cedar) helps to protect stored wool clothing and linens. When necessary, cedar blocks can be sanded down to restore the fragrance.

Closed storage Cabinets, cupboards, and shelving concealed behind doors are referred to as closed storage. Closed storage can hide untidy tangles of electronics or everyday household goods.

Cove lighting Concealed light sources discretely located behind a cornice or horizontal recess, cove lighting reflects light from the ceiling and illuminates the architecture of a room.

Creamware Made of light-colored clay and fired with an almost colorless glaze, creamware was developed in England in the early 1700s and was, for the next one hundred years, the most widely used pottery in Europe. Wedgwood, who streamlined the classic forms, became its most prolific producer. Printed or painted patterns and borders were sometimes added to the simple shapes of the lightweight earthenware.

Curio cabinet "Curio" is short for "curiosity," and these narrow glass-enclosed cabinets are designed with several tiers of shelves to show off collections of unusual or rare items.

Custom storage Builders or cabinet-makers consult with a homeowner to design and build storage, such as shelves, bookcases, and cabinets, to fit specific needs and spaces in a house. The most expensive choice among storage options, custom storage is tailored to the household's needs.

Daybed A chaise longue on which one can recline at full length. It is large enough to convert into a bed when needed. It may have arms at either end or a chair-back at one end.

Decanter An ornamental glass vessel designed for holding liquid, traditionally wine poured from a bottle. Early English and Irish decanters came in a variety of shapes, including square sided.

Dressmaker's form As they sewed, seamstresses once fitted clothes on a dressmaker's form, or dummy, usually a soft, fabric-covered torso on a wood pole set on a base. These forms are ideal for displaying vintage clothing and accessories and other distinctive outfits.

Eaves The overhang of a roof beyond the facade of a building. Inside the house, slanted space beneath the eaves is often a good place to install storage.

Ebonize A treatment to stain wood flooring or furniture black. The process was developed to mimic ebony, a dark tropical wood. This finish was especially popular during the Art Deco period.

Enamelware Metal dishware coated in thin layers of enamel – a smooth, glassy glaze. Enamelware is suited to storage outdoors or in humid areas such as the bath because it is durable and rustproof.

Film reel canister A flat tin cylinder designed to hold movie reels.

Fitted storage Storage designed to slot into a particular space. Unlike built-ins, which are constructed on-site, fitted storage pieces are made elsewhere and adjust to the right size and shape.

Gallery A room or hallway where art collections or photos are displayed. Galleries – initially without the art – appeared in grand European houses between the sixteenth and eighteenth centuries as long hallways where owners and visitors could exercise during cold or rainy weather. Residents soon began to line these walls with paintings.

Galvanized Metal coated with a thin layer of another metal, such as zinc, for added rust resistance. Storage containers made of galvanized metal work well outside or in humid environments.

Glazed tile These ceramic tiles are pressed into molds and fired with a glassy coating. This process seals the porous clay, making glazed tiles water resistant and easy to clean.

Graduated storage Containers or shelves of varying sizes, stacked or lined up from smallest to largest in order to make the most of a tight space.

Halogen A modern refinement of the incandescent light bulb, these lamps are filled with halogen gas and offer bright, white light, compact size, energy efficiency, and a longer life than incandescent bulbs. Halogen creates less of a yellow cast than incandescent bulbs, so color reads truer to natural light.

Hatbox Containers constructed of cardboard with cylindrical, hexagonal, or octagonal sides. Designed to hold the hats women once regularly wore and traveled with, hatboxes offer whimsical storage possibilities and stacking options.

Ladder-back chair The back of this chair looks like a runged ladder, with several horizontal slats between two uprights. One of the best-known examples is the Shaker chair, an elongated version of earlier British country ladder backs.

Lazy Susan A revolving circular tray originally intended to sit on a dining table and rotate a selection of relishes, condiments, and the like. These days, a lazy Susan might store a rotating collection of dishware and other household items within a cabinet.

Limestone A relatively soft rock mostly composed of calcium carbonate, which comes from the organic remains of shells and coral. Builders use the soft grayish or beige stone for countertops, fireplace surrounds, and walls.

Long-term storage applies to items kept out of circulation for longer than six months, such as out-of-season clothes, old tax records, and other household goods that are only occasionally used. An attic, basement, or crawlspace may be the best location for long-term storage. Cedar chests, hangers, blocks, or balls keep insects away, and archival boxes prevent the deterioration of paper. In a basement that tends to be humid, a dehumidifier or at least a low-wattage light bulb with a pull cord is helpful.

Mahogany A reddish brown hardwood that becomes deeper and richer in color as it ages. Prized in interiors for its durability and in furniture making for its varied, beautiful grain, mahogany was first imported to England from the West Indies in the 1700s. Its use grew so widespread that the dining table was commonly called "the mahogany."

Media center Also known as an entertainment center, a media center consolidates electronic equipment and related materials in one place. Well-ventilated armoires, cabinets, and shelving are a few of the options for gathering home electronics.

Modular storage Components that come in standard sizes and are designed to be combined to suit specific needs and spaces. Modular shelves and containers are more flexible than built-in or fitted storage and can be moved easily and added to when necessary.

Mudroom A less formal entrance to the house and a place to keep outdoor clothing and gear for inclement weather. A mudroom is generally situated just inside the back door or off the kitchen.

Open storage Shelves, cubbyholes, and other storage systems that are open to view. Showcase good-looking books, dinnerware, and objects in open storage to make it double as display. Traditional Shaker societies hung hats, brooms, and even chairs along walls on rows of pegs.

Ottoman An upholstered, backless stool or seat that is highly adaptable and can double as a low table or a footstool. Named for the Ottoman Turks and popular since the early eighteenth century, the ottoman arrived at its current form during the Victorian era.

Pegboard Fiberboard building material with evenly spaced holes for holding hooks, shelves, or pegs. Tools or other items hung from the hooks or stacked between pegs remain easily visible and accessible. Pegboard can be found in sleek, metal versions as well.

Polaroid Trademarked name for instantly developed photographs taken with a Polaroid camera. Useful for cataloging the contents of storage containers, Polaroids can be taped to the outside of a box or kept in a notebook as reference.

Redwood While any wood that produces a red dye is considered a redwood, the most famous are coast redwoods, which grow up to 360 feet in height. This durable hardwood is used in home interiors and exteriors, including the housing of spa tubs, decks, siding, paneling, and rustic furniture.

Secretary A compact desk with a top section for books and a writing surface that closes up to present a smooth, uncluttered front. Developed from portable writing desks, secretaries originated in England and America in the seventeenth and eighteenth centuries.

Shadow box A shallow, closed-frame box that allows you to display and protect three-dimensional artwork, books, or mementos behind glass.

Steamer trunk A piece of luggage designed to accompany travelers on transatlantic steamship crossings in the early 1900s. Custom fitted with a variety of compartments, a classic luxury steamer trunk had sections for suits, coats, shirts, shoes, linen, a hat, walking stick, and umbrella. The drawers and cubbyholes are ideal for storing clothing, jewelry, and accessories.

Terra-cotta Meaning "baked earth," terra-cotta existed as early as 3000 B.C., when it was used to make pottery vases and statuettes. Its use as an architectural material dates back to ancient Greece, when terra-cotta roof tiles and decorative elements adorned temples and other structures. Today, tiles made of this natural material are a popular flooring option. Whether glazed, painted, or unglazed, they add warmth and rustic charm to their surroundings.

Treasure wall A display of mementos inspired by Chinese curio cabinets, such as those in the National Palace in Beijing's Forbidden City, where several cabinets set together display noteworthy carvings, vases, and other objects. The shelves of these Chinese cabinets abandon the traditional grid arrangement and instead are irregularly spaced.

Trug A shallow, oblong gardening basket with a handle. Originally made in Sussex, England, of wide willow strips and used to measure grain and animal feed. These carryalls are frequently made of wood and used as rustic and portable storage.

Vitrine From the French for "pane of glass," a showcase or cabinet made of glass panels, which is used for displaying special items such as dishes, glassware, artifacts, or any collection of objects.

Wicker Created by weaving flexible branches or twigs from plants such as bamboo, cane, rattan, reed, or willow around a coarser frame, wicker is commonly used to make durable baskets and furniture. Wicker baskets offer attractive storage solutions. A durable material, wicker can last up to a century in normal use.

Wire-gauge shelving This style of sturdy, metal industrial shelving originated in warehouses, hospitals, and restaurants. The wire's gauge ranges, but is generally hefty and designed to hold heavy loads. Usually sold as a modular system, wire-gauge shelving is available in both polished and vinyl-coated styles.

Wool damage Wool moths are small and pale golden, with a wing span of about one-half inch. These moths damage woolens when they are in the caterpillar stage, but can be discouraged by dry-cleaning clothing before placing it in storage, and by including cedar products in storage boxes and closets. Exposing clothing to sunlight, heat of 110 degrees Fahrenheit for thirty minutes, or freezing temperatures for seventy-two hours also kills wool moths.

Wrought iron A commercial grade of iron that is bent into shape to create decorative and durable architectural elements such as grates, furniture, wine racks, and stair railings. Decorative forms include Gothic tracery, plant forms, and classical motifs. Today, wrought iron is sometimes actually made of steel.

Zoning Dividing a room or space into zones or sections reserved for different purposes with the help of furnishings, lighting, or accessories. For example, a great room might have zones designated for dining, relaxing, or watching TV.

Index

A

accessories, 94, 120–21, 122–23
apothecary bottles, 156
appliances, 77
architectural salvage, 49
artwork
  books as, 45
  displaying, 52–53, 54–55, 137
  hanging, 53, 54
  lighting for, 55
attics
  storage in, 175, 176, 179
  as workspaces, 175

B

baskets
  under bed, 100, 103
  for books, 50
  in entryways, 26, 180
  in kitchens, 80
  in wall displays, 18
bathrooms
  built-in storage for, 129, 131
  designing storage for, 127
  displays in, 138, 146–47
  family, 134, 137
  guest, 149
  master, 129, 131, 138, 145
  shared, 127, 129, 131, 138, 141–42, 145
  zones in, 129, 134, 139, 142
bath supplies, 127, 131, 146–47
bedrooms
  displays in, 93
  lighting for, 100
  maximizing storage in, 93, 95, 100
  multi-use furniture in, 94
  organizing, 96, 100, 103
  zones in, 103
beds
  for display, 93
  storage under, 93, 96, 100
benches
  in bathrooms, 142, 145
  in entryways, 26
  in mudrooms, 180–81

C

cabinets
  bathroom, 129, 134
  family room, 60, 62
  kitchen, 77, 88
  for media storage, 69
cake stands, 72, 140-41
CD collections, 59, 66, 69, 70
cedar balls, 117
chairs, ladder-back, 149
chalkboards, 38, 86, 148
china, 77, 79
cigarette boxes, 95

bins, plastic, 134, 137
blankets, 99, 104–05
blue
  with blue-green and green, 159
  with white and honey, 115
  with white and taupe, 137
bookcases
  built-in, 16, 18, 40, 43, 47, 51
  installing, 40
bookplates, 38
books
  antique, 45
  displaying, 38, 40, 45, 50
  first-edition, 73
  hardcover, 45
  leatherbound, 45
  organizing, 38, 50–51, 59
  shadow boxes for, 45, 73
  shelves for, 40, 43, 51
  stacked, 38, 50, 96
boots, 29, 121
botanicals, 49
bottles
  apothecary, 156
  caddies for, 71
  drying racks for, 87
boxes, archival storage, 21
brown
  with white and mahogany, 21
  with yellow and red, 45
brushes
  paint, 173
  scrub, 159

clipboards, 86, 155
closets
  accessories for, 109
  converting, into laundry room, 160
  customizing, 118–19
  dressers in, 110, 112
  linens, 104–05
  organizing, 109, 112, 115, 118–19
  replacing doors of, with fabric, 117
  scenting, 105
  storing clothes in, 109, 112, 116–17, 122–23
  walk-in, 110, 112, 115
clothespins, 159
clothing
  closet storage for, 109, 112, 116–17, 118–19, 122–23
  coats, 29, 123, 181
  dresses, 123
  entryway storage for, 29
  hangers for, 109, 110
  hats, 93, 116
  laundry room storage for, 153
  long-term storage for, 123
  mittens and gloves, 29, 180
  mudroom storage for, 180–81
  neckties, 117
  outerwear, 29, 123, 181
  repair station, 112, 155–56
  shoes and boots, 29, 33, 111, 115, 118, 119, 120, 121
  skirts, 123
  socks, 162
  suits, 123
  sweaters, 115, 123
  trousers and pants, 123
coffee mugs, 87
coffee tables, 60, 97, 98
collections
  arranging, 18
  of books, 38, 40, 43
  media, 66, 69, 70–71
  shadow boxes for, 46
color-coding systems
  for storage containers, 60

color palettes, 21, 29, 49, 65, 69, 85, 99, 103, 115, 133, 137, 145, 173, 179
compotes, glass, 147
cookbooks, 86
cosmetics, 94, 131, 145
creamware, 87
crystal, 79
cubbies
  for coats, 181
  in kitchens, 83, 88
  in mudrooms, 181
  for treasure walls, 46
cupboards
  lining, 104
  organizing, 60, 131
curtain rods, 118–19

D

desks
  customized, 43, 62, 170, 176
  leatherbound accessories for, 45
detergents, 156, 159, 160, 162
dining rooms, 77
dishes, 77, 79, 83, 88
displays
  of artwork, 52–53, 54–55
  balancing, with storage, 13–14, 16
  in bathrooms, 141
  in bedrooms, 93
  of books, 38, 40, 45, 50
  in family rooms, 72–73
  in hallways, 30
  in kitchens, 77, 80, 86–87
  ledge, 73
  in living rooms, 37, 38, 40, 45, 46, 49
  of mementos, 46, 72–73
  of photos, 18, 21, 30, 52–53, 72–73
  on staircases, 53
  strategies for, 14, 86
  on walls, 18, 52–53
documents, 179
drawers
  for accessories, 122
  for books, 50
  for CDs, 70
  for linens, 105

lining, 88, 104

organizing, 131

scenting, 105

for socks, 162

dressers, 110, 112

dresses, 123

dressmaker's forms, 93, 116

duvets, 103

DVD collections, 59, 66, 69, 70–71

E

enamelware, 146

end tables, 96

entryways

functions of, 25, 26

importance of, 25

organizing, 32–33

storage in, 25, 26, 29

espresso

with white, 133

with white and red, 69

F

fabric softeners, 156, 160, 162

family bathrooms, 134–37

family history, 52, 72

family rooms

displays in, 72–73

functions of, 59

media collections in, 66, 69, 70–71

open vs. closed storage in, 66

organizing, 59, 60, 62

zones in, 62

faucets, 131

file folders, 69, 70

film reel canisters, 66, 71

first editions, 73

flower market carts, 176

flower pails, 156

flowers, 87

focal points, 18

folding tables, 153

frames, 18, 21, 52, 72

furniture, multiuse, 60, 95

G

games, 59, 66

gardening tools and supplies, 173

glass

compotes, 147

containers, 131

displays under, 16, 72

jars, 117, 155

storing, 79

vases, 72, 146

vitrines, 16

gloves, 29

gray

with white and stainless steel, 179

green

with blue and blue-green, 159

with honey and latte, 103

grooming accessories, 131, 133, 141

guest baths, 149

H

hallways, 30

handbags, 93, 121

hangers

clothing, 109, 110, 117, 123

for pictures, 54

wooden clip, 53

hats, 27, 28, 93, 116

holiday ornaments, 179

home offices, 62

honey

with green and latte, 103

with red and stainless steel, 173

with white and blue, 115

hooks

in bathrooms, 142, 149

in kitchens, 88

in mudrooms, 180, 181

I

ironing board, 153

irons, 159

ironstone, 49

islands, 83, 88

J

jars

glass, 117, 155

jewelry, 93, 94, 95, 120

K

keys, 24, 26, 29

kitchens

customizing storage in, 79, 80, 83, 88

displays in, 77, 80, 86–87

eat-in, 77, 80, 83, 85

islands in, 83, 88

open vs. closed storage in, 77

zones in, 80, 83

knives, 85

L

laboratory glass, 120

landings, 30

laundry notebook, 160

laundry rooms

hideaway, 160

organizing, 153, 163

stain removal center in, 153, 155, 156, 163

storage in, 153, 155–56, 159, 162–63

leather

leatherbound books, 45

leatherbound desk accessories, 45

ottomans, 38

ledge displays, 73

libraries, 38, 40, 43, 45

library tables, 43

lighting

for artwork, 55

for bedrooms, 100

for laundry rooms, 153

for utility rooms, 167, 170

limestone, 83, 129, 145

linens, 79, 85, 104–5

living rooms

books in, 38, 40, 43, 45, 50–51

functions of, 37

photo and artwork galleries in, 52–55

M

magazine racks, 62

magazines, 66, 69, 137, 145

mahogany, 129

mail

mailboxes as containers, 155

place for, 32, 33

master bathrooms, 129–33, 139, 145

media

centers, built-in, 46, 48, 60, 62

organizing, 66, 69

storage for, 59, 70–71

mementos

displaying, 46, 72–73

storing, 179

mirrors, 30

mittens, 29, 180

movie collections, 59, 65, 66, 69, 70–71

mudrooms, 180–81

music collections, 66, 69, 70–71

N

neckties, 117

newspaper clippings, 70

night tables, 95

O

offices, home, 61, 62, 170, 175, 177, 178

organization

importance of, 13–14

ornaments, holiday, 179

ottomans, 38

P

paintbrushes, 173

pants, 123

papers, 179

pegboard

for drawer liners, 88

for tools, 168

pewter, 141

photographs

albums for, 69

arranging, 18, 21, 52–53, 72–73
copies of, 52
family history in, 52, 72
framed, 18, 21, 52, 72
in hallway displays, 30
hanging, 53, 54
lighting for, 55
loose, 21, 66, 71
in staircase displays, 53
in a timeline, 53
pillows, 99, 103, 104
plants, 62, 87
plastic
  bins, 70, 134, 137
  jars, 155, 159
plates, 77, 79, 80, 83, 88
postcard racks, 73
pots, 26
potting shed, indoor, 173

R

red, 168
  with honey and stainless steel, 173
  with white and espresso, 69
  with yellow and brown, 45
remote controls, 71
room dividers, 134

S

scrub brushes, 159
secretary desks, 95
sewing kits, 156
shadow boxes
  advantages of, 73
  for books, 45, 73
shaving supplies, 145
shelves
  for books, 40, 43, 51
  color of, 46
  floor-to-ceiling, 110
  in hallways, 30
  recessed, 129
  reclaiming space in, 13
  for treasure walls, 46
  wire-gauge, 176

shirts, 119, 123
shoes
  closet storage for, 111, 115, 118, 119, 120, 121
  entryway storage for, 29, 33
silverware, 79
skirts, 123
slipcovers, 100, 103
soaps, 133, 146, 147
sock drawers, 162
spa, home, 138
spice racks, 168
stain removal products, 153, 155, 156, 163
staircases, 30, 53
steel, stainless,
  with red and honey, 173
  with white and gray, 179
stereo equipment, 59
storage
  in attics, 175, 176, 179
  balancing, with display, 13–14, 16
  in bathrooms, 127, 129, 131
  in bedrooms, 93, 94
  in closets, 109, 112, 116–17, 118–19, 120–21, 123
  color-coding, 60
  in entryways, 25, 26, 29
  in family rooms, 59, 60, 62, 66, 69, 70–71
  in kitchens, 77, 79, 80, 83, 88
  in laundry rooms, 153, 155–56, 159, 162–63
  in living rooms, 37, 38, 43
  master log of, with photographs, 179
  for media collections, 70–71
  open vs. closed, 66, 77, 127
  reclaiming space for, 13
  strategies for, 13–14
  in utility rooms, 170, 173
suitcases
  storing, 121
  vintage, 93, 175
suits, 123
sweaters, 115, 119, 123

T

tables
  custom, 167, 176
  folding, 153
  library, 43
  work, 167, 170
tableware, 77, 79
taupe
  with white and blue, 137
  with yellow and cherry, 145
telephone table, 32
televisions, 46, 59, 62, 62, 66
toilet paper holders, 137
tools
  care for, 173
  pegboard for, 168
toothbrush holders, 146
towels, 137, 139, 145, 148–49
toys
  in family room, 59, 62, 65
  for tub, 137
trays
  for bathrooms, 139, 145, 149
  roll-out, 96
  spa, 138
  wooden, 103
treasure walls, 46, 49
trousers, 123
trugs, wooden, 80
trunks, 93
tubs, 142
TVs, 46, 59, 62, 66

U

umbrella stands, 181
utility rooms
  creating, 167, 168
  functions of, 167, 168
  lighting for, 167, 170
  organizing, 167
  storage in, 170, 173

V

vanities, 95, 112, 129, 141, 142
vases, 21, 72, 146
video collections, 59, 65, 69, 70–71
video games, 59
vitrines, 16

W

walk-in closets, 110, 112, 115
walls
  of books, 40, 59
  cubbies in, 46, 168
  for displays, 18, 52
  treasure, 46
white
  with beige and stainless steel, 179
  with blue and honey, 115
  with blue and taupe, 137
  with brown and mahogany, 21
  with espresso, 133
  with gray and natural, 29
  with red and espresso, 69
  with sage and wheat, 65
  with wheat and khaki, 49
window seats, 37, 88, 142
wine crates, 175
wool sweaters, 115, 119
workrooms, 168
worktables, 167, 170

Y

yellow
  with red and brown, 45
  with taupe and cherry, 145

Z

zoning
  for bathrooms, 129, 134, 141
  for bedrooms, 103
  for family rooms, 62
  for kitchens, 83

Acknowledgments

Project Editor
Laurie Wertz

Copy Editor
Peter Cieply

Designers
Marisa Kwek
Jackie Mancuso

Illustrators
Paul Jamtgaard
Nate Padavick

Indexer
Ken DellaPenta

Photography Assistants
Robert Cardellino
A. J. Dickson
Stephen Funk
Marc Horowitz
Marco Walker

Stylist Assistants
Shaz Arasnia
Darlene Dull
Greg Lowe
Jackie Mancuso
Frank Millero
Rob Oxenham
Joshua Young
Karen Zambonin-Young

Lead Merchandise Coordinator
Tim Lewis

Merchandise Coordinators
Andy Brown
Peter Jewett
Mark Johnson
Dan Katter
Peter Martin
Nick McCormack
James Moorehead
Paul Muldrow
Grady Schneider
Mario Serafin
Roger Snell

Weldon Owen thanks the photography and editorial teams for their creativity and stamina in producing this book and acknowledges the following people and organizations for their invaluable contribution in:

Allowing us to photograph their wonderful homes
Howard & Lori Backen, Cindy Brooks & Judith Thompson, Pamela Fritz, Robert & Kelli Glazier, Susie Heller, Cynthia & Michael Karasik, Lisa & Corey Kliman, Elaine Nelson, Jill Poole, Rod Rougelot and his canine wonder Becker, Jessica Seaton & Keith Wilson, Reesa Tansey & Gary Greenfield, Celia Tejada, and Norma & Robert Wells

Supplying artworks or props
Joshua Ets-Hokin (ETS-Hokin Studios, San Francisco), Danette Ferro (Nordstrom), Pamela Fritz, Joan O'Connor (Timeless Treasures, San Francisco), Gaines Peyton (Sears-Peyton Gallery), Reesa Tansey, Celia Tejada, and Sheri Sheridan (Swallowtail)

Catering on location
Kass Kapsiak and Peggy (Catering by Kass), and Andrew Mayne, Frederick Scott, and Arlene Susmilch (Stir Catering)

Providing assistance, advice, or support
Nola Anderson, David Armario, Jim Baldwin, Emma Boys, Garrett Burdick, Julie Dodge, Betsy Gammons, Mary Ann Hall, Ron Hampton, Holly Harrison, Tom Hassett, Sam Hoffman (New Lab), Anjana Kacker, Anna Kasabian, Emily Noh, Pottery Barn Creative Services, Tam Putnam, Jason Stewart, Mary Silver, Sara Terrien, and Juli Vendzules

Author Acknowledgments
No project of this scope is accomplished without the contributions of many people. We wish to thank our editors, Shawna Mullen, Laurie Wertz, Sarah Lynch, and Peter Cieply.

All photography by Stefano Massei, except for:
Jacket front cover, photography by Alec Hemer. Page 67, image on flat-screen TV courtesy of The Kobal Collection.

All styling by Deborah McLean, except for:
Pages 2, 15 (top and bottom left), 16–21, 30 (right), 31, 32 (left), 38–45, 50, 51 (right), 52 (left), 53 (top), 60–65, 70 (top and left), 71 (right), 72–73, 80–85, 86 (top left), 87 (right), 92, 100–103, 104 (right), 108–15, 116 (right), 117 (left), 134–37, 146 (right), 147 (left), 148 (right), 149 (left), 154–61, 162 (bottom left), 163 (left), 166, 180 (right), 181 (right), 188, styling by Alistair Turnbull. Pages 36, 51 (left), 52 (right), 58, 66–69, 70 (bottom right), 71 (left), 126–33, 147 (right),168–73 styling by Thea Geck. Jacket front cover, Page 1 styling by David Benrud. Pages 10–11 styling by Greg Lowe. Page 173 (bottom) styling by Michael Walters.

About Pottery Barn

Founded in 1949 as a single store in Manhattan, Pottery Barn has evolved into America's leading source for style. For more than fifty years, Pottery Barn has brought comfort, style, and inspiration to people who love their homes. You can shop from Pottery Barn by calling 1-800-922-5507, by visiting us online at www.potterybarn.com, or by stopping by a store near you.